Linda

Please share with y-

Best of love to both

Best Regards,

Tracy

MW01097405

The Harvester

Cover design by Maeve O'Regan

ISBN-10: 1519749546
ISBN-13: 978-1519749543

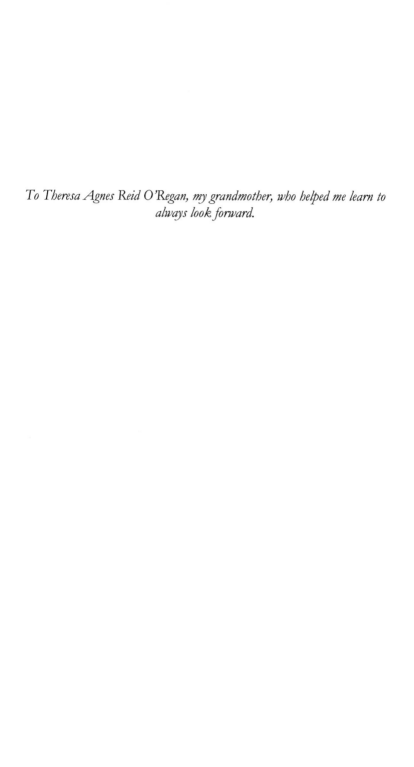

To Theresa Agnes Reid O'Regan, my grandmother, who helped me learn to always look forward.

Contents

Acknowledgements

To my family and friends, to the families who have lost someone to brain cancer, and to those who are fighting it, please know: Have faith. I do believe there is a place and time for you to develop your faith: whether it is through God, your friends and family, or from something you don't yet know about. Try believing. Faith will make you a stronger person, as it did me.

To Chris, Dad and Mom, Heather and Travis, as well as Pam, Todd, Mignon, Haley, and Grant – thank you for always being there for me. To my aunts, uncles, and cousins – thank you for always having my back. And to my best friends from Colchester, Vermont, and from my college days at the University of Vermont and the University of Texas School of Law, who told me I was tough enough to fight this cancer – thanking you is not enough to acknowledge all that you have given me.

I also want to thank the people of MD Anderson – the doctors, nurses, and staff who guided me through my fight, even when the outcome didn't look so good.

Lastly to Rob O'Regan, my uncle, who convinced me that my story was worth telling: I will never forget what you've given me. By helping to share my journey with others, you have shown me what true family means. Grandma is so proud of all of us.

To anyone who is fighting brain cancer, or any other form of the disease, I truly hope that my story will help. I wish you Godspeed in your fight.

Prologue

Faith of the Harvester

The Gaelic name "Toiréasa" – Theresa – means "harvester." Curious, I researched the meaning of "harvester" and found it defined as someone who harvests or gathers. Gathers what, I wondered. Food? Wine? Money? Or was it something more? I dug a little deeper and found that while harvesting usually pertains to the gathering of crops, it can also refer to acquiring achievements. Still curious, I looked up "achievement" and found what I was looking for: "a great or heroic deed." It was there that I started to understand my grandmother, Theresa Agnes Reid O'Regan.

It was late December 2002 when I got the call from my mother. I was at the office, getting ready to leave for my law firm's Christmas party. Mom was crying. "Tracey, she's not doing well," she said, referring to her mother and my grandmother. "You need to get up to Vermont to say your goodbyes." Stunned, I hung up the phone and immediately called Chris, my husband of four months.

"Babe, I just got a call from my mom," I told him. "It looks like Grandma's not going to make it much longer."

My grandmother, Theresa, was an eighty-two-year-old resident of Colchester, Vermont, a small town on the shores of Lake Champlain. My mom and dad had settled in Colchester in November 1976, and Grandma and her husband, Patrick, had relocated there when they retired to be closer to their grandkids. (I was the oldest of what would eventually become a brood of thirteen offspring of Terry and Pat's six children.) A widow since my grandfather had died a decade earlier, Grandma had narrowly escaped death herself in 1998 when she lost control of her car as she was driving back to her apartment and hit a tree head-first.

Her health in the four years since hadn't been great. But her trip to the emergency room on December 16, 2002, after a night of vomiting, was still unexpected.

A day later, the news was even more stunning: The doctors discovered that Grandma had an advanced stage of ovarian cancer, and her health was declining quickly. That's when Mom made calls to her kids – Heather, Travis, and me – to tell us we needed to get to Vermont. It wouldn't be easy. We all had settled into our own lives at that point and were spread across the southern United States. I was in Houston with Chris, embarking on a new law career. Heather was in Atlanta with her husband, Adam, and their daughter, Alexandra. Travis was a grad student at Ole Miss in Oxford, Mississippi. We were all preparing to head to our parents' home in Roanoke, Virginia, in a week to celebrate Christmas, but those plans would have to be put on hold.

"Do you want to leave tonight?" Chris asked. "I can book us a flight right away – it's up to you."

"I think we need to be up there," I said, tears rolling down my face.

"Well then, you head home, pack for us both, and I'll make the reservations."

Hanging up the phone with Chris, I wiped the tears from my eyes and went looking for one of the firm's partners to tell him I was going to miss the Christmas party. I walked down the hallway at Beck Redden & Secrest, a boutique trial law firm in Houston that I had joined in September, and found Tom Ganushaue, one of the junior partners. Tom was a true gentleman from Louisiana, a Catholic like me, and when I told him why I had to leave, he said simply, "Godspeed."

◊◊◊

Until that cool December evening, 2002 had been the most amazing year of my life.

On January 15, I turned thirty. It was a meaningful milestone for me. My childhood had been a mixed bag, filled with a lot of self-doubt despite being raised in a warm and loving family, with plenty of friends in picturesque Vermont. I had worked extremely hard to overcome my lack of confidence, and by the time I turned thirty, I had turned things around. I finally felt like I understood who I was and what I wanted.

Four months later, on the eleventh of May, on a beautiful spring day in Austin, Texas, I graduated from the University of Texas School of Law. I had taken one huge step closer toward my childhood dream of becoming a lawyer.

I immediately began cramming for the bar – while also planning a wedding. On the seventeenth of August, I married my true love, Chris. We spent the next month in Europe on our honeymoon.

On September 29, I found out I was pregnant. Chris and I were going to be first-time parents! I was stunned, thrilled, and terrified all at once.

The next day was my first as an attorney at Beck Redden. I had interned there during my last summer of law school, and was one of five associates the firm hired that fall. There I was, dressed sharply in a brand-new black blazer and skirt, pink silk blouse, and black pumps, settling into my office at one of the most prestigious corporate litigation firms in the region, just two doors down from one of the founding partners. Chris had just opened his new office in the same building, so he helped carry in my box of "stuff." We were both extremely proud.

I had finally found perfect harmony in every aspect of my life. Everything that I had dreamed of, prayed for, and busted my ass to achieve had all fallen into place over the course of the past year.

And then in the blink of an eye, everything changed. My life was about to take a turn that I could neither comprehend nor stop.

◊◊◊

After saying goodbye to my colleagues at the firm, I went home and began packing for the trip to Vermont. Chris arrived shortly thereafter, changed from his suit and tie into jeans and a sweatshirt, and we headed to the airport.

Our flight from Houston to Burlington, Vermont, took us through Pittsburgh, where we had to change planes. As it turned out, Heather, who booked a flight from Atlanta after receiving Mom's call, was also connecting through Pittsburgh. We met in the boarding area. Heather was traveling with one-year-old Alexandra, who is also my goddaughter. Heather was pregnant with baby number two, and like me was due the following spring. Heather's pregnancy wasn't going nearly as well as mine had to that point – lots of morning sickness and the tossing of cookies that goes with it. The headaches I was having seemed minor by comparison.

I sat next to Heather on the plane, with Alex on my lap, so Heather could get some rest. We were in the very last row of a puddle-jumper. Chris sat on the other side of the aisle. During the flight, when I wasn't keeping Alex distracted, I kept thinking about Grandma. I was her first grandchild. We had lived apart when I was a toddler, but after she and my grandfather had moved to Vermont after retirement, I saw her at least once a week – at church, for dinner, or at one of my many swim meets or field hockey games. She was always in my life. Even when I moved out of Vermont and began my journey as an adult, our connection remained strong.

That connection continued, somewhat unbelievably, after Grandma passed away two days before Christmas.

Chapter 1

Growing Up

I was the first child of William and Virginia Hilton, born on January 15, 1972, in Portland, Maine. Mom and Dad had met in the early 1960s when they both lived in nearby South Portland. Dad was a native "Mainiac" while Mom had grown up in New York City before her parents moved the family – three girls and three boys – to South Portland in 1962. Bill and Ginnie began dating in April 1963 and were still a couple when Bill deployed to Vietnam in October 1966 as a member of the U.S. Army Special Forces. The Special Forces – known as the "Green Berets" because of their distinctive headgear – is an elite group of soldiers that specialize in guerilla warfare.

On July 5, 1967, Dad's unit was deep in enemy territory when he was shot while on a mission. He's the first to admit that he never should have made it home alive. He credits the "montagnyards," the local mountain dwellers who helped the Green Berets in the fight against the North Vietnamese, with saving his life and bringing him back to his unit's base camp. But he had lost a significant amount of blood, and was touch and go as plans were made to evacuate him and the other wounded soldiers. Days later, as he was being transferred to a military transport that would take him back to the States, a doctor ordered that he be taken off the plane for treatment, convinced that he wouldn't survive the flight home. The Army actually lost track of him for a while at that point. His parents were distraught – and furious. His dad, Charlie Hilton, called one of Maine's U.S. Senators at the time, Ed Muskie, to get answers. When Muskie said he couldn't help, my grandfather followed the chain all the way up to the office of Vice President Hubert Humphrey, demanding to know where his son was. Bill was finally located at a military hospital in Japan, and he eventually was cleared to fly back to the States. He arrived at Valley Forge Hospital in Virginia in September 1967 – three months after being wounded. He had lost most of his right leg, from just above the knee, and would face a lengthy rehab and many more surgeries. But he was alive.

Bill and Ginnie stuck together through this crisis. They were engaged in November 1968 and married two months later at St. John the Baptist Church in South Portland. In 1972, Mom gave birth to me. Dad had left the military and was working his way up the ranks at a fast-growing department store chain called Zayre. Being a retail manager enabled Dad to pursue a variety of opportunities across the chain of stores across the New England region – which means we moved frequently. I was in Maine for two whole weeks before we began our journey as retail vagabonds. Our first stop was Enfield, Connecticut, where we lived for two years. Then we hopscotched across three Massachusetts towns – Pittsfield, Holyoke, and Agawam – from 1974 to 1976. Each stop formed bits and pieces of my personality.

As an infant, I cried a lot – an awful lot, according to my mother. As it turned out, I had a good reason: I was allergic to the formula I was taking! Once Mom switched to another brand, I was fine. Call it the first life test that I had to overcome.

Mom says I was very lovable – what would you expect a mother to say? – but also a bit reserved, even as a toddler. There was a time when I was two or three that Mom put me on a Ferris wheel expecting that I would love it, but instead I sat there, stone-faced. I didn't cry, but I didn't smile either – I just sat there, looking like I was bored. Afterward, Mom cried because I showed no emotion while on this great ride!

I have some fond memories of those early years. I loved playing house. I had a toy stove and refrigerator in our Pittsfield house. I would also play in the cabinets where Mom kept the pots and pans. I would crawl in there with my blanket and my dolls and have a grand old time. My blanket was my constant companion growing up. I even took it with me to college. There wasn't much left of it by then other than some tattered threads, but I needed it with me.

Shortly after I turned four, my parents put me in the Miss Jones Story Book Nursery School, in Holyoke. There were no children my age in our neighborhood, so my parents thought preschool would be a good place for me to meet new playmates. I took a school bus, three days a week. I remember two friends – a redheaded boy who my mom remembers as devilish, and a Japanese girl who I loved playing with.

The first house my parents purchased was in Agawam in 1976. I hated living there. The kids in the neighborhood were mean to me, and eventually I stopped playing with them. That may have been the beginning of my insecurities about my appearance.

I was three when my sister Heather was born, and we were living in Pittsfield. Like most firstborn children, I was not happy having to share my parents' affection with a new sibling. My parents like to tell the story about when they returned from the hospital with Heather. I was on my tricycle at the top of the driveway, which sloped down to the street. I was wearing a pair of black patent leather dress-up shoes that I was not allowed to wear outside. When my parents pulled into the driveway, I started coasting down the pavement on my bike – dragging my feet the entire way to scuff the toes of the shoes. That was my way of showing how unhappy I was with the new arrival.

After Heather was born, my role changed. I was expected to help a lot, even though I was only three years old. I was always a bit of an "adult," wise beyond my years. Mom likes to say that I was fifteen when I was born because I always enjoyed talking with adults – and bossing my sister and brother around. Maybe that's why I got along so well with my grandmother, Theresa O'Regan – Mom's mother.

Our family didn't have a lot of money, but we would always take a family trip every year. One of my favorites was the summer after first grade when we went to Disney World in Florida with my friend Jenni Miller and her family. It was an amazing trip, in part because it was our last vacation with the Millers before they moved to London. In 1981, we visited the Millers there. It was a crazy time to be in London, with the Royal Family grabbing headlines. Prince Charles had just announced his engagement to Lady Diana Spencer. Later, back home, I sat transfixed in front of the TV watching the Royal Wedding – along with 750 million other viewers across the globe – as Charles and Diana were married on July 29 at St. Paul's Cathedral in London.

Our family traveled to Maine a lot. When I was four and Heather was a baby, my parents rented a cottage on Moosehead Lake, about a four-hour drive northeast of Portland. My grandparents and two uncles planned to stay with us as well. It was a very rustic setting – the cottage was right on the lake, in a remote area accessed by a dirt road. There was no plumbing and the electricity was supplied by a gas-powered generator in an adjacent shed. The first day Dad, Grandpa, and Uncle Brian left the cottage to go shopping for supplies. Mom, Grandma, Uncle Rob (Mom's youngest brother, who was fifteen), and the girls stayed behind to unpack. Even though it was midsummer, it was chilly on the lake and the men fired up the generator to heat the cottage before they left.

After they'd been gone for a while, the generator started making a terrible, loud banging sound, and thick black smoke began pouring out of the shed. We thought it was going to explode. The cottage had no phone (and this was the pre-cell phone era), so Mom and Grandma gathered up the kids, jumped in the car, and headed into town to find help. As we were driving out of the campsite, Dad, Grandpa, and Uncle Brian returned. The cars pulled up next to one another and Mom frantically explained what was happening. The men raced back to the cottage, and we turned around and followed behind. Back at the cottage, Uncle Brian and Dad opened the shed door and more smoke billowed out. They covered their mouths against the thick, dark smoke, stepped into the shed, and shut down the generator. They fixed the exhaust hose that had become detached and got the generator running again. The incident turned out to be a bad omen, as the rest of our vacation contained more than our fair share of accidents and poor weather. But for years we've always laughed at the infamous Moosehead Lake Vacation.

The trip wasn't a total disaster, however. It was the first time I remember riding on a boat. The lake water splashing in my face and the breeze whistling in my ears felt magical.

In 1976, close to my fifth birthday, our family moved to Vermont. My parents bought a three-bedroom split ranch on a dead-end street in Colchester, a suburb of Vermont's largest city, Burlington. Our neighborhood abutted the Winooski River, which feeds into Lake Champlain, where we would spend many glorious summer days swimming or on the motorboat Dad bought after we settled into the community. The recently developed area was bustling with new families raising their young children. I met my two best friends – Jenni Miller and Hannah Schwartz – at preschool, and we remain close to this day. We did everything together – rode bikes, played tag, swam, and just hung out – from morning until night.

When I was in the first grade, Mom and Dad signed me up for a swim team at Marble Island Resort, a marina and nine-hole golf course on Mallet's Bay. Marble Island was owned by a wonderful man named Fred Fayette and his brothers and sisters. The seven summers we spent on Marble Island were the best. I made new friends there. I learned to swim, experiencing the sheer joy of jumping off the dock into the lake, over and over again, with my friends, Heather, and Travis, our brother who was born in 1979. I took swim lessons every weekday morning and then spent the rest of the day around the resort with my friends – swimming, boating, playing on Thayer's Beach, and, on rainy days, playing cards or games in the Marble Island clubhouse.

Dad bought our first family boat when I was in the fifth or sixth grade. He asked me to go with him on the maiden voyage on Lake Champlain. I was so proud! We launched at the bottom of the Winooski River, close to our house. I was so excited that we finally had our own boat – until Dad asked me to steer while he looked at a map. I was terrified! I saw a boat heading in our general direction – a safe distance away – but panicked and told my dad it was time for him to take the wheel.

I learned to golf on Marble Island, and spent almost every summer day running around the golf course in search of lost balls. My dad moored the boat at Marble Island, and we spent countless hours tubing, waterskiing, or just motoring around the lake. Dad had a knack for finding a quiet spot to anchor the boat so we could swim and have a relaxing lunch.

Every August, the family would drive up to Dartmouth College in New Hampshire for Heather's and my final swim meet of the summer. From there we would continue to Maine and stay at my dad's old house on Tremont Street in South Portland, where his parents and brothers and sister still lived. Grammy and Grampy Hilton were always happy when I saw them. We'd all spend time together on the beach, visiting Two Lights State Park on the Atlantic Ocean in Cape Elizabeth. During these trips, I learned to love lobster. I watched Dad and Grampy play cribbage. And I learned how parents could still love their kids even when they *may be* misbehaving.

Swimming was a great activity for me during the winter months. And I started playing field hockey in the fall. Sports definitely helped me get through an odd period of my life when I began feeling insecure.

As a preteen I began to feel fat, even though my parents and doctor never considered me overweight. Every time I looked in the mirror, I was filled with self-doubt about my weight and general appearance – more than a "normal" kid probably experiences during the preteen years. It didn't help that Heather was blond and thin and beautiful.

Despite a loving family and strong friendships, I began to feel like an outsider. My middle school years were a horrible time for me socially. But I compensated for my insecurities by studying hard and getting good grades. I felt like I needed to be perfect in school to make up for my physical shortcomings. I always did my homework without being asked and turned my projects in early. Putting so much effort into school often left me exhausted by the time I got home, and I needed my space. As much as I liked playing with my friends, I was just as happy to sit inside all day and read a book. I never got into trouble, which had a lot of other parents asking their kids, "Why can't you be more like Tracey?"

In the fifth or sixth grade, I first started thinking about and talking about becoming a lawyer. What sixth-grader does that? I was very goal-driven, and practicing law was one goal I set for myself early on. I must have talked about it a lot, because on our first home computer, Heather printed out a sign that said *The Law Office of Tracey Hilton*. Years later, after I graduated from law school, my parents framed the printout and gave it to me as a gift. When I started at Beck Redden & Secrest in 2002, I hung the sign in my office.

Our family loves to laugh. The summer after I graduated from eighth grade, Mom and Dad told us they had bought tickets to an air show in Burlington, and our friends the Schwartzes were going too. The movie *Top Gun* had come out in May and I had a huge crush on Tom Cruise. But at fourteen, my friend Hannah Schwartz and I were too cool to go to an air show with our parents, so we stayed home and hung out with the other kids in the neighborhood. We were in front of a friend's house when our parents returned from the air show. "Tracey, you have to see what you missed!" Mom said. Hannah's dad Mike pulled out a picture of Tom Cruise in his Top Gun uniform, with a handwritten message:

"Tracey, sorry you didn't make it you the air show – Love, Tom Cruise."

I wanted to cry. I thought my life was ending! After I moped around the house for a few days, someone finally told me the picture was a hoax. All I could do was laugh. Oh, how I love my family, and the Schwartzes, too!

◊◊◊

I learned a lot of valuable lessons from my mom and dad, as most kids do. One particular moment with Dad stands out. In high school, things started to click for me, physically and mentally. By my senior year at Colchester High School, I was a co-captain of the varsity field hockey team, president of the student council, and a lifeguard and swim instructor at Colchester Park on Mallets Bay. I even had my own car, a 1982 stick-shift VW Rabbit. Life was good.

CHS had a program each fall called Laker Spirit week, when the school would celebrate one of the fall sports teams: boys' and girls' soccer, cross-country, and field hockey. During Spirit week, captains of the fall teams were allowed to read the morning announcements over the school intercom.

The field hockey team was honored the week of an important home game. It was such a big game that our principal, John Willard, canceled the weekly staff meeting so the teachers could attend the game. Unfortunately, only three teachers showed up to cheer us on. We won the game, but I was livid.

I was scheduled to read the announcements the next morning, and I took advantage of the opportunity to share my frustration with the entire school. I read through the normal announcements – the day's weather report, the lunch menu, and the winning score from our game. And then I ad-libbed: "We would like to thank the THREE teachers who came to the game – and for the rest of you who decided not to attend, you missed a REALLY good game." I slammed down the handset and stomped to my AP History class. As I was leaving the office, I could hear a teacher telling Mr. Willard that I had "crossed the line" and "disrespected" the staff.

I was taking a test in History class when Mr. Willard entered the room. "I need Tracey to come with me to my office," he said. I was mortified. The teacher, Mr. Kish, interrupted and told Mr. Willard that he would send me to the office after I finished the test. As I handed the test to Mr. Kish, he said, "Tracey, it's okay to fight for what you believe in."

When I entered the principal's office, Mr. Willard was clearly upset. He demanded that I apologize to the teachers. Remembering what Mr. Kish told me, I told Mr. Willard that I would not apologize. I started crying and told him I needed to talk to my dad. I called Mom and asked for Dad's work number. (Mom was on the Colchester school board and I didn't want to involve her in this mess.)

I called Dad's office and his assistant, Mary Ann Barcomb, answered. She could tell I was crying. Dad was in a meeting, so she put me on hold for what felt like days. She came back on the line and transferred me to Dad. I told him what I had done and that I was in trouble.

Dad left his meeting and drove to the high school. I met him outside. It was a crisp, sunny day with the beautiful fall foliage peaking. Dad and I talked for about an hour. He reinforced what Mr. Kish told me – that it's important to stand up for what you believe in, despite what others are telling you. When you do that, he said, you start to figure out who you really are.

Dad also suggested that I write a letter to the teachers to explain my actions. He was big on being accountable. I stayed up late that night writing the letter. I explained that I spoke up because I was disappointed that so few of them supported our team. I also made a point to say that I was *not* apologizing. I delivered the letter to Mr. Willard the next day. Some of the teachers never really forgave me – and I was fine with that. It was an eye-opening few days for me, and I learned a lot about myself.

◊◊◊

There's one more enduring memory about my childhood in Colchester. A commercial building owned by a company called Ladd Research abutted our neighborhood. The company developed electron microscopy supplies for researchers. It was a strange building – set back in the woods, at the end of a dead-end street, on the banks of the Winooski River. We used to cut through the property on our bikes to go to the general store. Some nights we'd play flashlight tag there. One time Hannah looked through the window and saw a monkey in a cage. They were testing animals! We freaked out, took off running and screamed all the way home!

There were many stories told by the neighbors about how the company dumped chemicals regularly on the grounds around the property. The Environmental Protection Agency eventually listed Ladd as a hazardous waste handler. In the late 1990s, the business relocated to nearby Williston. The Vermont Agency of Natural Resources was asked to inspect the site in advance of the sale of the property. Testing turned up low levels of several contaminants, including cancer-causing elements called Polycyclic Aromatic Hydrocarbons, but the levels were not significant enough to raise any red flags. The agency could not determine whether the contaminants were caused by Ladd or occurred naturally. It also noted that the sandy makeup of the soil made it likely that any contaminants would have been quickly flushed into the Winooski River below – where we and many other families spent endless summer days swimming.

As cancer coursed through our neighborhood, our suspicions grew. During or shortly after the time Ladd was operating on that site, at least forty-seven people in our neighborhood were diagnosed with cancer. The list included my mom, who battled breast cancer in 1986.

I often wonder if that's when the tumor started forming in my brain.

Chapter 2

A Special Bond

Theresa Agnes Reid O'Regan was a bit of a renaissance woman, albeit one wrapped in a shroud of devout, conservative Catholicism. Born on August 22, 1920, she was raised in Queens, the easternmost of the five New York City boroughs. Despite the financial devastation the Great Depression brought on her parents, Theresa entered Queens College at the tender age of seventeen and was a member of the college's first-ever graduating class in 1941. Her commitment to attending school and graduating during the height of the Depression was an early sign of the fortitude she would show later in life.

Theresa – friends called her Terry – loved dining and dancing. She enjoyed drinking (vodka martinis) and smoking (menthols) – both in moderation, of course! After graduation she landed a job as a "skipper" in the Admirals Club of American Airlines at a municipal airport in Jackson Heights, New York. She met her future husband, Patrick Pearse O'Regan, while working at Macy's in Herald Square over Christmas vacation in 1941. Pat worked in the men's department and was beginning a lengthy career in retail – a career that would soon be interrupted by World War II.

Soon after the Japanese attack on Pearl Harbor, Pat enlisted in the Army. He was trained in construction by the U.S. Army Corps of Engineers and sent to Canada to work on the Alaska-Canada (AlCan) highway project in the spring of 1942. The 1,500-mile road was built to facilitate the flow of supplies to the Alaskan defenses against the Japanese.

Corporal O'Regan spent eleven months in Canada, at which point he evidently had enough of enlisted life. He was accepted to

Officer's Candidate School and left Alaska for training at Camp Fannin, Texas. He took a brief detour to Queens to marry Terry on March 27, 1943. Their honeymoon was brief – two nights at the Hotel St. Moritz, overlooking Central Park – since Pat was scheduled to report to Camp Fannin on April 9. Their first son, Patrick Jr., was born on April 26, 1944, and six months later, Pat Sr. shipped overseas with the rest of the 410th Infantry Regiment of the 103rd Division to join the war in Europe. The Division fought in France and Germany until May 8, 1945, when the German High Command surrendered and the war in Europe officially ended. Pat returned to the States in late 1945, and was released from active duty in January 1946.

Terry and Pat – mostly Terry – would eventually raise six children in a two-bedroom apartment in the Parkchester neighborhood of the Bronx. Their first daughter and second child, Virginia, is my mom. In 1962, with the Bronx taking a turn for the worse and the family having vastly outgrown its accommodations, Terry and Pat packed up their kids and their belongings and moved to South Portland, Maine, where Pat had taken a job with a local department store chain called Zayre – the same retailer my dad would join a decade later.

After the family moved to Maine, Terry learned to drive. She also took courses to become a practicing speech and language pathologist for physically disabled children and young adults. She worked at the Cerebral Palsy Center in Portland and tutored many disabled children from her home. Terry also loved writing poetry – and was pretty good at it.

Her passion for words and speech extended to another cornerstone of her life: the Catholic Church. She volunteered as a lector for many years in the towns she lived in: South Portland; Portage, Michigan; Atkinson, New Hampshire; and, finally, Colchester, Vermont. Terry loved speaking in front of an audience – and was wonderful at it. She spoke clearly and passionately, especially from the lectern at Sunday mass. (She always let her fellow lectors know that she expected the same passion and enunciation from each of them.)

Terry was gracious in that old school, cosmopolitan kind of way. She was the epitome of Tom Brokaw's book *The Greatest Generation*. She credited a lot of her personality to her mother, Eleanor (Conroy) Reid. I don't remember much about Eleanor, my great grandmother, since I was only three years old when she passed away. Eleanor was the daughter of Irish immigrants who was born in Omaha, Nebraska. Our family never quite understood how the family ended up in Omaha, until my mom discovered a book titled *Orphan Train*. Written by Christina Baker Kline, the book chronicled the life of a young lady who traveled from Ireland during the potato famine to the Eastern United States. Many young Irish immigrants were sent to the Midwest to assist the farmers. That's probably the path Mary Greene, Eleanor's mother, and Mary's future husband, Thomas Conroy, took. We can only speculate that Mary and Thomas were relocated orphans who met in Nebraska, married, and gave birth to Eleanor before moving back to New York City. I love tracing my family history, but we don't know much more about my great grandmother's family. One keepsake that Grandma gave me is a glass cup with these words: "1906 Narragansett Pier, May Green." Grandma told me that despite the misspellings, the cup belonged to Mary Greene, my great-great grandmother.

My only lasting memory of Great Grandma Eleanor was visiting her in a nursing home with Mom and Grandma in Scarborough, Maine; it must have been shortly before her death. She was in her late eighties at the time and not doing well. The nursing home had a horrible smell – I thought I was going to throw up! I remember helping to carry in some body powder –

the kind that women in the 1970s used to smell "pretty." Grandma and Mom both had great respect for Eleanor, and I wish I had the chance to get to know her.

◊◊◊

Grandma's relationship with me, her firstborn grandchild, was different than the ones she shared with the rest of her grandkids. I just loved that woman. She wrote this poem for me shortly after I was born:

> Dear tiny Tracey Anne - your life has just begun
> May your future be as bright as the rays of the Sun
> May your faith stay with you for the rest of your life
> Giving you true joy in the Happy Days
> Strength and comfort in times of strife ...
> God bless you first grandchild with your precious baby smile
> We have found every moment has all been worthwhile.

The bond she and I shared had many layers – it was educational, and spiritual, and at an elevated level, in terms of discussing books and poems and her education. My mom is a fantastic mother, but when I was younger she and I didn't always see eye to eye on some of the things that were important to me at the time. But Grandma and I always did. We could sit together all day reading books. Other kids in the neighborhood would be out playing, and Mom would nag at me for not being outside with them. But I liked hanging out with Grandma.

There was this: Grandma gave me my first pair of see-through nylons. I was in third grade, and Mom always insisted that I wear white or black tights – no skin tones. But Grandma bought a pair for me even though she knew Mom wouldn't approve. I guess that's part of a grandmother's duty. She did things like that, things that told me she understood me in ways that no one else ever did.

When Grandma and Papa (that's what I called Grandpa O'Regan) moved from Michigan to New Hampshire in 1978, I was able to spend a lot more time with them. Whenever we visited their house in Atkinson, I would spend some time reading whatever Grandma was writing. They had a table in their living room, just to the right of the second-floor stairs, which was where Grandma did her writing. She always had piles of papers on the desk, filled with poems and stories and other things she was working on. She would let me go through all of them, and I'd ask questions about her writing.

She inspired me to start writing poems myself. Poetry gave me a way to express myself, to talk about some of the things I was feeling at that age that I couldn't explain verbally. I kept a book filled with many of the things I wrote. A lot of the poems were goofy, nonsensical, such as "The Old Man":

> There was an old man
> Who lived in the zoo.
> One day he lost his shoe
> While feeding the elephant in the zoo
> "Pick up your shoe," said the elephant to the man
> "I cannot do so," said the old man,
> "The snake next to you has taken it."
> "What should I do?" asked the old man.
> "Talk to the snake," the elephant told the old man,
> "I cannot do so," said the old man,
> "Because he is now eating you!"
> The next thing he knew the snake had taken the elephant and his second shoe!
> The old man ran, not even thinking about his shoe
> And never went back to the zoo.

I wasn't always happy growing up. Writing funny things kept me laughing.

In 1984, after Papa retired, he and Grandma moved to Colchester. I was thrilled! Grandma began attending all of my field hockey games. She was always there to cheer me on. She'd yell louder than anyone, even though that woman knew nothing about field hockey!

Grandma supported me, but that didn't stop her from getting on my case from time to time – especially about religion. She was a devout Catholic. She never missed Sunday mass. She was a proud member of the Catholic Daughters and managed the Lectors at Holy Cross Church in Colchester. That's one of the things we disagreed about. She wanted me to be a lector, and I had no intention of getting up in front of a congregation and reading Bible verses. My decision clearly hurt her feelings. One night, when we were together for dinner, I made it worse.

"I don't believe in all of the things about the Catholic Church," I told Grandma. Mom was there too, and they both looked at me like I had killed a cat. I tried to recover: "Just because I don't believe in everything the Church says doesn't mean I'm not a faithful Catholic," I reasoned. It was too late. In Grandma's mind, the damage was done.

◊◊◊

Grandma was far from perfect. She did frustrating things, especially as she got older. She was a classic dawdler. It would often take her several minutes from the time she picked up her purse to the time she actually left her apartment. "Where are my reading glasses?" she would ask no one in particular. She would grab extra tissues. She would look for her car keys. She would tell a story. It was always something. Her pace could be very frustrating – especially to Mom, who spent more time with her than anyone in the months after Papa died in late 1992.

Papa went into the hospital in December of that year, shortly after his seventy-third birthday. His health had been in decline for some time. He was overweight, and after decades of smoking he had been diagnosed with emphysema He became less and less mobile, and one day his lungs became so congested he could no longer breathe on his own. Grandma, in a panic, called my parents, who called for an ambulance – and then raced to Grandma and Papa's house across town so they could follow the ambulance to the hospital.

At the time, I was a junior at the University of Vermont, in nearby Burlington, and I was the only grandchild who could visit Papa in the hospital (my siblings and cousins were too young). I would take him for walks in his wheelchair, because he was no longer strong enough to walk on his own. As his condition worsened, he wasn't able to talk anymore. Sitting in his wheelchair, he would simply reach back, grab my hand, and hold on tight as I pushed him slowly through the corridors. Given his condition, we knew these were his last days, and that he would probably never leave the hospital.

One day when I visited, Mom and Aunt Eileen were there, but Grandma was not. They were upset with Grandma because she hadn't arrived yet – she was out running errands or something, and they felt she should be there because Papa was so ill. But I believe Grandma felt helpless because her husband was dying and she couldn't do anything about it. She didn't know what to do or how to act around him. So she made herself scarce.

Later in the day, when Grandma finally arrived, she looked at him lying there, virtually lifeless in the bed, and she started crying. As quickly as she had entered the room, she turned around and walked out the door. She walked down the hall to compose herself. I felt so bad for her.

Papa died on December 18. His funeral was a few days before Christmas. I don't remember the mass, but I do remember the burial. Burials were rare in Vermont in the winter, because the ground was generally too frozen for the gravediggers. But we had a warmer winter in 1992, so Papa's burial took place in a cemetery next to a small military base in Colchester. The ground may have been soft, but the weather was freezing cold and windy that day. None of Papa's grandchildren knew what to do during the brief ceremony at the gravesite. This was the first death in the family that any of us had experienced. We just stood there, watching Grandma and her six children place roses on his casket. Finally, I put my hand on the casket and said, "I love you, Papa." The rest of my cousins did the same.

◊◊◊

It took Grandma awhile to get over Papa's death. But in many ways his passing liberated her. My grandfather was never an easy man to live with, and his declining health made him even grumpier. He often took out his frustrations on Grandma, and she took the verbal abuse quietly, as a good wife did back then.

When he passed, Grandma mourned, and at times talked of her loneliness. But she survived, and eventually settled into her independence. She sold the house she and Papa shared and moved into a two-bedroom apartment in a new senior housing complex behind Holy Cross Church. Granted, the move to a smaller apartment wasn't easy, as she eloquently summarized in a poem titled "Downsizing":

That's what I'm told
I should be doing...
Like corporations-
"Pare down."

"Let's go."
"Sort out."
"Toss the excess."
"Cut the clutter."
"Rid your life of STUFF!"

But I'm not a corporation-
Not a CEO.
Just a sentimental Mom and Grandma;
Widowed now.
How do you "pare down"
letters of love over the years-
Through war and peace?
How do you "toss"
precious photos, homemade cards,
poems composed by your children,
artwork drawn by tiny hands?
The loss might be too much
for me. I think.

I try to comply —
To simplify.
Unlike the corporate firms —
with each decision
I die a little.
And I cry ... a lot.

But the transition opened new doors for her. She made new friends. She organized outings and various projects for members of the housing complex. She began traveling more and enjoying time with her growing brood of grandchildren. Her fifteenth, Conor, was born in 1998, the year I turned twenty-six.

Then she had a car accident that nearly killed her.

◊◊◊

On October 13, 1998, Grandma was driving home at dusk after an afternoon of shopping. She was less than a mile from her apartment when she apparently fell asleep at the wheel, veered off the road, and hit a tree head-on. Later, she would tell the story of a "guardian angel" – a young EMT named Debbie – who was driving behind her when the accident occurred. Debbie immediately pulled over and comforted the battered, bloodied elderly woman until the ambulance came.

Grandma's injuries were massive: fractures to her pelvis, left shoulder, ribs, cheekbone, and left heel, along with numerous facial lacerations. Because of her age – she was seventy-eight – the surgeons didn't think she'd make it through the night.

At the time of the accident, I was in Evansville, Indiana, on a work trip. Mom called to tell me about Grandma's accident, and I caught the first available flight back to Burlington. Arriving at Fletcher Allen Hospital, where my dad worked, I made my way to Grandma's room in ICU. As I walked into the room, I was hit by the same acrid odor I had smelled two decades earlier in the room of my great-grandmother's nursing home. I could feel it – Grandma was dying.

Approaching her bed, I could see that her face was swollen, almost unrecognizable. She wore a neck brace, and blankets covered her severely bruised and bandaged body. A breathing tube prevented her from speaking. There was terror in her usually radiant blue eyes. I'm sure she felt as if she were dying – but it was also clear she was not okay with that. She grabbed my hand, squeezed it tightly, and mumbled my name around her breathing tube. We were both crying.

It was a short visit. I held her hand for a bit longer, then kissed her and said, "I'll be right back, Grandma." I joined my family in the hall and tried to suppress the nausea I was feeling.

I stayed for a couple of days before returning to Indiana; I had to get back to work. Other family members were saying their goodbyes to Grandma – no one really thought she was going to pull through at that point – but I just didn't believe that it was her time. I did not feel that she was on her way to heaven just yet.

She proved me right. Eventually, her condition stabilized, and the doctors were able to begin performing the many surgeries she would require to mend her broken body.

Months later, while in rehab, Grandma wrote a poem called "Dream Sonnet" recounting those first few hours in the ICU:

> *She dreamed as she had never dreamed before*
> *As she had never dreamt she could or would.*
> *Reality had flown to distant shores*
> *A fantasy was all she understood.*
> *With body weightless as feathers of down.*
> *She soared to secret places of her mind.*
> *Tossed by turbulent waters, would she drown?*
>
> *In this nebulous world, what would she find?*
> *Was she alone, lost in a foreign land?*
> *A soul lost in a labyrinth of pain.*
>
> *She sensed a Presence, felt a gentle hand;*

And knew that she would wake and live again.
Miracles still happen. Faith can amaze.
The Lord God works in mysterious ways.

◊◊◊

Grandma survived, but her body would never be the same. She had to learn to walk again as her old bones healed – some more slowly than others. The next time we were together was at Heather's wedding in 1999. Grandma was just learning to walk again, first with a walker and eventually with a cane. Although she seemed miserable – sore, tired, and unhappy that she could no longer drive – she was thrilled to be at a family gathering. And though she could barely walk, she danced at the wedding. She always loved to dance.

Several months later, I was back in Vermont for a close friend's wedding. I traveled to Burlington a few days early and spent the day before the wedding with Grandma – just the two of us. We went shopping and had lunch at a local restaurant by Lake Champlain. We talked and talked – about my first year of law school, about her recovery and rehab, about anything and everything. It was perfect.

In May 2002, Grandma flew to Austin to attend my graduation from the University of Texas School of Law. I was so proud that she was there – and she was clearly proud of what I had accomplished. This was all somewhat ironic, since Grandma had never encouraged her own three daughters – my mom, middle daughter Moira, and the youngest girl, Eileen – to attend college. Coming from someone who herself graduated from Queens College, our family always considered her attitude toward her daughters quite conservative. But as she got older – and after Papa died – Grandma's attitude seemed to become more progressive. She wanted all of her grandkids to be happy and successful, regardless of whether they were working or unemployed, married or single, gay or straight. She was fiercely protective and exceedingly proud of all of us.

And if you're curious, I'm still writing poetry.

Chapter 3

Perfect Harmony

The four years following Grandma's accident were an incredibly busy time in my life. Chris and I started dating in early 1998, after he left the staffing company where we first met. He was my boss, and I was one of his key players – the division I ran was the only one turning a profit when he joined the firm in July 1996. After Chris left a year and a half later, the firm should have promoted me into his district manager position, but they didn't – I suspect it was because I was young (just twenty-five at the time) and a woman. I left shortly thereafter, to join First Institutional Marketing Inc. (FIMI), which was one of the staffing firm's commercial banking clients. I received both my Series 7 and Series 56 licenses so I could sell securities and other investment products; my job as a marketing director involved training bank personnel to sell annuities and similar financial products.

One night in the spring of 1998, Chris and I were sitting outside my small apartment on Richmond Avenue in Houston's Westchase District, about 10 miles from my office. We were having wine, cheese, and shrimp, and discussing our life goals. I confided that I had always wanted to be a lawyer.

"So why don't you go to law school?" Chris asked.

"It's too late for that," I replied.

But he wouldn't let it go. "If that's what you always wanted to do, then you should do it," he said.

His push was enough to convince me to take the LSAT and apply to law schools. I was visiting my family in Vermont at the time the LSAT was available, so I took the test at the University of Vermont, where I had graduated four years earlier. I was so nervous I didn't even say goodbye to Mom as I left the house – I just hopped in her car and drove away. Despite my anxiety, I scored pretty well on the test – well enough to apply to five law schools: the University of Houston Law Center, the University of Texas School of Law, University of Miami School of Law, George Washington University Law School, and Notre Dame Law School. All but George Washington accepted me. I chose Texas because it was the highest-ranking law school of the four. I began a three-year program in the fall of 1999.

Based on my background, I thought I would be best in bankruptcy law. That type of law consists of a little bit of arguing and a whole lot of research. During my second year of law school I landed a summer associate program with a bankruptcy law firm. But one of the partners called me in February 2001 and informed me that the firm was splitting up and they weren't going to have any summer associate openings. That was seriously bad news, because by that time all the other firms had their associates locked in for the summer. I searched high and low for an opening at another firm but had no luck. My friend George Hittner, who I sat next to for the majority of law school (bound alphabetically by our last names, Hilton and Hittner) were talking one day and he suggested that I call his dad, David Hittner, a federal judge for the Southern District of Texas for whom I had interned the previous summer. I frantically called him to see if he knew of any law firms in the area that were still looking for summer associates. He requested my resume and made a few calls on my behalf. The judge knew one of the partners at Beck Redden & Secrest and recommended me. My summer associate position at Beck Redden set the ball rolling for me to land my unexpected dream job – as a trial lawyer. Later that summer, Beck Redden made me an offer to join the firm after I graduated. I was thrilled!

◊◊◊

In December, I was invited to attend the firm's Christmas party, and asked Chris to go with me. Little did I know what he had in store. He had bought an engagement ring and was trying to find the right place and time to propose. When he found out the Christmas party was at the Museum of Natural Science in Houston, he called Alistair Dawson and Joe Redden, two of the partners at the firm, and asked permission to use the setting to propose to me.

Unbelievably – considering that I hadn't even started working yet – both Alistair and Joe said yes.

Chris came up with a grand plan to put the ring in its own display case in the gemstone exhibit. He received permission from the museum's curator and created an exhibit called the "A Green Mountain Diamond" – in honor of the Green Mountains of Vermont, where I spent most of my childhood. Chris and a few of his friends spent days building this "exhibit" – it even had an illuminated case. He put the ring in the case along with its own description. For two days, the exhibit was in public view, available to anyone visiting the museum.

On December 21, the day of the party, Chris added a red rose to the exhibit. He had spoken with a security guard at the entrance to the gemstone room, asking that once he and I went in, no one would be allowed to follow. It was our moment.

At the party, I was speaking with Joe Redden when Chris walked up and said, "Hey, Joe! Mind if I take Tracey for a minute?" I was horrified – Joe was one of the two big dogs at Beck Redden, and I was not even an official attorney yet. Unbeknownst to me, Joe was in on the surprise. He said, "Sure, go right ahead."

As I gave Chris the evil eye, he whisked me away and led me to the gemstone exhibit. We began working our way around the room, pausing to look at each display case. By this point, Chris was so nervous he was focusing primarily on trying not to throw up, but I didn't notice. Finally – it must have seemed like forever to Chris – I reached the case holding the Green Mountain Diamond, which for obvious reasons had caught my eye. I began to read the description about the display diamond's "history":

*This particular gem has experienced quite a journey. Originally discovered in its raw form in Maine, it was quickly moved to Vermont where it began to take shape. The gem of "H" color continued to grow in carat weight during its early years, with its **VS1** clarity taking shape in the **Vermont Sun.***

Over the years the gem was cut and polished until it relocated to Houston, Texas where it continued to take shape, developing additional facets all along the way. For what seemed like an eternity the gem vanished, then surfaced in Austin, Texas. Once located it took 3 years to return the gem to those in Houston who loved her.

The "Green Mountain Diamond" is a very rare and special gem whose unique and special qualities are rarely found in nature individually. Please take a moment to admire her, for she is something to behold.

This beautiful 1.4-carat gemstone is on loan and will be on display through December 21, 2001.

A few seconds in, it hit me. There was a beautiful diamond and a red rose in front of the placard. I turned to my left, with tears in my eyes, and Chris was down on one knee. "Tracey, will you marry me?" he asked. I was crying – and hyperventilating a bit – but managed to say yes. Chris reached into his pocket, pulled out the key, unlocked the case, and took out the ring. He slipped it onto my left ring finger.

Meanwhile, the rest of the party guests had gathered at the entrance to the exhibit, with champagne flutes. As we walked out, they toasted us. I was overwhelmed.

◊◊◊

Our engagement was just the kickoff for the whirlwind year that lay ahead. In January 2002, I turned thirty. It was a milestone that unofficially signaled the transition from my old self – self-conscious Tracey Anne – to the person I always wanted to be.

I didn't have much time to reflect, however. In addition to finishing my last semester of law school, I had an August wedding to plan. And oh, we bought a house too – a model home in a new development in Humble, Texas. It definitely qualified as a dream home: 4,300 square feet, five bedrooms – even a wine cellar! It was beautiful. We didn't need to move in right away, so we leased it back to the builder, who would continue to show it as a model home for the next two years. Chris and I had one stipulation: Our wedding ceremony and reception would be held there. We signed the papers on the house in June.

On May 18, I graduated from the University of Texas School of Law at the Sunflower Ceremony. I was so very proud to receive my law degree. Mom and Dad flew in from Virginia. I was thrilled that they were there to share this special moment with me. They had been through so much together and had taught me so much about life, about pursuing my dreams. Both had inspired me over the years in their own way.

It was Dad who taught me how to deal with adversity. If I was having a fight with Heather, or I had a problem with school, he and I would talk it out and find the best way to deal with it. He showed me how to understand any problem I was having, how to address it, and most importantly how to move on. Here's just one example: I was never a good math student. In seventh grade, I had a horrible teacher, which compounded the challenge. Every night, when Dad got home from work, we'd lie on the floor in the family room and go through that day's math assignment until I understood it. That's how I got my grade up from a D to a B.

Mom instilled her own brand of toughness in me. When I was twelve years old, she was diagnosed with breast cancer. I was terrified that she was going to die. But she fought, and she survived, and I learned what would be an invaluable lesson about not giving in to cancer.

Mom and Dad were joined at my graduation by Heather, who came from Atlanta, and Travis, who made the trip from North Carolina where he was a senior at Elon University. Chris was there, of course, along with his stepmother Pam, who came from Indiana. Aunt Eileen (Mom's sister) came with Grandma from Vermont. It was a big trip for Grandma, since her mobility was severely limited following her car accident. She required special orthotic shoes because her foot and heel bones had been crushed. As a woman who was always conscious about fashion, she really hated those orthotics. She walked with a cane and always seemed to be in pain – her feet, or her shoulder, or her pelvis, all of which were shattered four years earlier when her car hit that tree.

Receiving my law degree was one of the highest moments of my life. Everything was falling perfectly into place. I had landed a job at a prestigious trial law firm that was a perfect fit for my interests and experience. And I was engaged to my best friend. Just a few years earlier, this all had been a dream.

After graduation, Grandma flew back to Virginia with my parents, and then we all met up again a week later at Travis's graduation from Elon.

Then it was time to cram for the bar exam. I had to take time off from the wedding planning to focus on the exam, which was scheduled for the last two days of July and the first day of August in Texas. I actually left Houston for two weeks before the bar to stay in Austin with my dear friend from law school, Jenny Salomon, so I would not be distracted. With the Beck Redden job starting in September, I couldn't afford to mess up. There were a lot of late nights – and a lot of headaches, which I attributed to the stress leading up to the exam.

There was no downtime after taking the bar. Our wedding was scheduled for August 17. The day turned out perfectly. We held the event at our gorgeous new house, and Judge Hittner performed the service. Many of our family and friends were there to share what turned out to be a fabulous night.

Two days later, Chris and I were off to Europe for a month-long honeymoon. The trip was wonderful. We flew into Paris, where we visited the Louvre and then took an evening boat ride down the Seine to see the Eiffel Tower, all lit up. After Paris, we visited Versailles, and then continued to Monte Carlo, Florence, Venice, and Lucerne, Switzerland. From Lucerne, we took a train to Munich, where we rented a car and drove through the Black Forest, visiting castles along the way. We ended our journey in northwest Germany visiting members of the Schoettelkotte family and driving down streets named *"Schoettelkotter Damm."*

We flew out of Frankfurt on September 7. Just a few days later I was on the road again, driving from Houston to Vermont for my childhood friend Hannah Schwartz's wedding to David Wood. I spent the first night in Memphis, then drove to Roanoke, Virginia, to visit Mom and Dad – and pick up some personal belongings that I wanted to bring back to Houston with me. That's why I drove instead of flying. Heather and Alex met me at our parents' house, and we drove together to Vermont. Mom and Dad flew up a few days later, as did Chris.

Hannah and David were married in Stowe, a popular Vermont ski town that is an absolutely beautiful place to visit in the fall. The day after the wedding, our family all went to my Uncle Brian and Aunt Susan's house in nearby Montpelier. Since most of my family in the Northeast couldn't attend my wedding, Brian and Susan offered to host a post-wedding reception for us.

During our stay in Vermont, Heather and I spent a couple of days with Grandma in her apartment next to Holy Cross Church. Grandma kept us up all night telling stories. She talked about growing up in New York City, and how she would go dancing in New Jersey after work at a nightclub where a young singer named Frank Sinatra performed regularly! We talked about politics, and her family – her parents, uncles, and aunts, many of whom I'd never met. That was when she gave me the red cup from her grandmother. The three of us laughed and laughed the whole night.

Neither Heather nor I knew it, but both of us were pregnant.

◊◊◊

After the party at Uncle Brian and Aunt Susan's, Chris and I made our way back to Houston. Playtime was over. I started at Beck Redden on September 30. I was one of five new associates to join the firm that year; one from was Harvard, one (the only other woman) was from Baylor, and the other three were from the University of Texas. The partners put us to work right away doing research, drafting documents, and attending depositions and hearings. It was a crazy atmosphere; most corporations don't bring on trial attorneys until the last minute, because they don't like paying the exorbitant fees. And Beck Redden & Secrest was expensive. But taking cases on right before trial meant a lot of catch-up work to prepare. That's what the associates were there for – and I absolutely loved it.

Working hard never bothered me. And this was my dream job. I loved the idea of practicing law. I loved being in front of a judge, asking questions in depositions, knowing that people were telling the truth or lying.

A week into the job, I found out I had passed the bar. What a feeling!

I finally was really happy, feeling great both mentally and physically. I was always an overweight kid growing up – at least in my own mind. I was never happy with me. But finally, I had reached a point where I was successful, I was feeling great, and I even thought I looked good. I had a lot of confidence and was in a great place. It was probably the best time of my life.

The day before I started work, I took a home pregnancy test, sensing that something was different. The positive result was a bit of a shock, considering the timing. I was locked in the bathroom at our house, trying to figure out how to tell Chris. As it turned out, I was needlessly concerned – Chris was thrilled. The final piece of our perfect year was in place: We were going to have a baby.

Chapter 4

Headaches

As a kid, I frequently had headaches, probably from the fifth grade on. They'd go away, then come back, and go away and come back again. I don't think I was ever tested for migraines or anything like that. They were just always there, and I dealt with them.

There were a few incidents in my twenties that should have been warning signs. But there always seemed to be extenuating factors. The headaches definitely got worse throughout law school. When I was studying for the bar with my friend Jenny in Austin, the pain was constant. I always attributed those headaches to the stress and fatigue of non-stop studying. Tylenol became my closest companion.

When I took the bar exam, I had trouble concentrating because my head hurt so badly. Thank God I passed.

When Chris and I were honeymooning in Europe, there was one day when I couldn't get out of bed because of a killer migraine. We were visiting Lucerne, but I wasn't up for sightseeing. Instead, I stayed in our hotel room for half a day with the shades drawn and the lights off. There were a few factors that I figured contributed to the migraine: our hectic travel schedule, being overtired, and maybe having had too much to drink the night before.

The headaches were more consistent after I became pregnant. I never had morning sickness or other nausea during my first trimester, but the headaches were horrible. Despite what seemed like constant pain, I never had any blackouts or fainting spells –

that is, until October of 2002, shortly after I started at Beck Redden & Secrest. I was neck deep in some research and had blown past lunch hour without eating anything – never a good idea for a pregnant woman. I finally realized how hungry I was, so I went to the cafeteria to grab a sandwich. (I hadn't been there long enough to know that the firm's administrative assistants would make those food runs for you!)

I was waiting in line to check out when I felt dizzy and fainted. I was out cold. Someone called an ambulance, and someone called Chris. The EMTs showed up around the same time Chris did. I was already feeling better, so instead of having the EMTs take me to the hospital, Chris and I decided it would be better to visit my new OB/GYN, Laurie Swaim.

Chris and I had already visited Dr. Swaim once to confirm the pregnancy. After my fainting episode, she did a bunch of tests on the baby, and everything looked fine. Dr. Swaim attributed the fainting to a combination of my pregnancy and not eating right. She told me to stop drinking coffee and to eat regularly, and sent us home.

Before the episode in the cafeteria, no one at the firm knew I was pregnant. I was nervous about telling the partners because I was so new. But after the fainting spell, we had to come clean. I was relieved that everyone was so supportive.

In early December, I was sitting in my office working at the computer. All of a sudden, the letters on the document I was typing became scrambled. I thought something was wrong with the computer. It stayed like that for about a half-hour. I tried to write using pen and paper instead, but I couldn't translate what I was thinking into words.

My head was pounding by this point, so I went home – I'm not sure how I made it – and went straight to bed. I never mentioned the incident to anyone.

Chapter 5

A Place in the Sun

For years, Grandma dealt with stomach problems. She was diagnosed in her mid-fifties with a peptic ulcer and had been on a variety of medications to treat her ailments. Maalox was a constant companion. She would alternately complain about phantom illnesses or downplay severe stomach pains. So in November of 2002, when Grandma told Eileen, her youngest daughter (and my aunt), about how much her stomach was bothering her, Eileen didn't consider it a big deal. Grandma had been going to physical therapy twice a week since her car accident four years earlier, and she had experienced near-constant pain in her left shoulder, collarbone, pelvis, and both feet.

On the morning of December 11, things got quite a bit worse when Grandma called Aunt Eileen and said she'd been up all night vomiting and didn't have the strength to get dressed. Eileen rushed to Grandma's apartment in Colchester and found her in the same clothes she'd been wearing the day before, covered in puke. She was dehydrated, weak, and in too much pain to clean up after herself. Eileen cleaned her up and called an ambulance.

The EMTs arrived and took Grandma to the emergency room at Fletcher Allen Hospital, a short drive away in Burlington. Our family has a long history with that medical facility, which dates back to the 1800s, when a local woman named Mary Fletcher funded the construction of one of the first hospitals in Vermont. My dad, after leaving the retail industry, had worked in Fletcher Allen's patient finance department for fourteen years before taking a job at Carilion Health System in Roanoke, Virginia, in 1996. And of course, my grandfather spent the last week of his life at Fletcher Allen in December 1992.

After arriving at the emergency room, Grandma was put through a series of tests that stretched throughout the afternoon and into the evening. Aunt Eileen's husband Gerry and my Uncle Brian had joined Eileen at the hospital. Just before midnight, the doctors discovered a large mass in Grandma's stomach. She was admitted shortly after midnight on December 12 – ten years to the day after her husband was taken by ambulance to the same hospital.

Grandma was diagnosed with a malignant ovarian tumor. The tumor had burst and was releasing toxins that were making her nauseous. The medical staff was pumping her with antibiotics and one doctor said the team would decide on a treatment once she started feeling better. Grandma turned to Eileen and rolled her eyes – as if she already knew what the outcome would be. This latest setback would be her last – after recovering from her car accident, she had no desire to fight another long battle, this time with cancer.

Eileen and Brian had begun calling their remaining siblings – Patrick, the oldest; my mom, the oldest daughter; Moira, the middle daughter, and Rob, the youngest – to update them on Grandma's condition. They all eventually made their way to Burlington after it became clear that the prognosis was grim.

We were all stunned. The cancer was completely unexpected. How could Grandma's personal physician have missed the tumor for so long? Eileen learned later, while cleaning Grandma's apartment, that she had scheduled an appointment in January for an ultrasound. Clearly, she knew something was wrong.

Our family began arriving on December 20. Mom and Travis were the first to arrive in Burlington, making the eleven-hour drive from Virginia. Heather and Alex flew up the next day from Atlanta, meeting Chris and me in the Pittsburgh airport, where we were catching our connecting flight from Houston. Heather's husband Adam drove from Atlanta to Roanoke and picked up Dad, and they drove to Vermont the next day. I admit I was a little grumpy – I thought Eileen was overreacting when she said we all needed to get to Vermont immediately. Why couldn't we wait until after Christmas? But by the time we arrived, I was thankful we had decided to make the trip.

Grandma, Heather, and I spoke a little when we first arrived. Unlike after her car accident four years earlier, she didn't look terrible. Her mood was fairly upbeat. Heather and I stood next to her bed, chatting and laughing for a few minutes before excusing ourselves so she could rest; she seemed very tired.

Later, back in Grandma's room, she turned serious. She held my hand tightly and asked, "Tracey, are you okay? You look upset about something." She seemed to sense that something was wrong. I told her I was fine, and that my pregnancy was going well.

It didn't take long for Grandma's physical and mental state to worsen considerably. The next day, she was drifting in and out of consciousness, in part because of the morphine she was receiving for the pain. She would talk from time to time, sometimes to her visitors or a nurse but often just speaking out, usually with her eyes closed, providing a steady stream of random thoughts and observations. Her sense of humor remained intact. At one point, she said she saw a "little man at the top of the stairs" who looked like Jay Leno. Later, she said a manager was watching over her, singing. "Where did he go?" she asked. "He has a business to manage." Her husband Pat was a department store manager for many years.

On December 21, after a few long shifts in the hospital's waiting room with my family, my head was really pounding. I was even having trouble remembering certain words. My mom thought it was because of the hormones from my pregnancy. And of course everyone made fun of me when I couldn't remember the word "bread" for the sandwiches we were making in the waiting room. That's our family – no one ever gets away with anything.

While I was forgetting words, Grandma was philosophizing about them from her morphine haze. "There are boxes filled with words, and one box holds a universal word," she said at one point. "And when you find that word, it will explain everything you need to know. And that will take care of it. There needs to be one universal word that everyone will agree on."

Our family spent a lot of time discussing what that universal word might be. I'm convinced she was talking about "faith" – one of the most important words in any language.

By December 22, the doctors had transitioned Grandma to palliative care, simply managing her pain. Her body had begun to shut down. Mentally, she seemed to be getting reacquainted with a few deceased friends and relatives, engaging in conversations that spanned two worlds.

"A lot of people are calling from upstairs," she said. She seemed to enjoy the interactions. "You've all got to stop imitating me!" she said. Later, she added, "Stop singing my birthday songs! It's my birthday – you can't start those songs without me."

But she wasn't quite prepared to join them. "Is that door open? Close that door!" she said. "I'm not ready to go yet!"

Gradually, however, Grandma began taking the next steps in her journey. Her faith in God gave her the strength she needed to embrace whatever lay ahead. Someone – she didn't say who – had a plan for her. "There's always someone watching you, and they're a reflection of everything you do," she said. "I think that's a good way to put it." Later, she added, "They said they wanted what's best for me, and now I'll have the perfect experience."

We were all curious about what Grandma was seeing in her quasi-dream state. Sometimes she would respond to our questions.

"I just saw heaven," she commented casually. "It's beautiful."

"What's so beautiful?" Eileen asked. "What did you see?"

"I saw wide-open fields – lots of greenery and all sorts of yellow."

Clearly, she knew what lay ahead, but she wasn't afraid. "I feel like I'm ready to get up, but I know I'm not," she said. "I'm ready to start moving forward." As her health faded further, she grew impatient. "Let's wrap this up instead of stretching it out," she said. "I'll be much better."

Later, while a nurse was checking her vitals, Grandma cried out, "Oh, dear Lord, merciful Jesus, help me! I'm ready to find my place in the sun."

"Can I get you anything, Mrs. O'Regan?" the nurse asked.

"Yes – a place in the sun!"

On the evening of December 22, Father Roger Charbonneau, Grandma's parish priest, came to visit. There were a dozen or so people in the room, and we all held hands as he led us in prayer. Then Father Charbonneau asked us to leave so he could spend some time praying alone with Grandma.

He was in there for a long time. After his visit, Grandma was much calmer, more at peace. And she let us know – in her own comforting way – that her time was near.

"I'm ready to say goodbye," she said, in a tone that was more of a sigh than a sentence. "Is everyone here? I'm very tired." We gathered around her bed and said our tearful goodbyes.

Mom, Dad, Heather, Travis, Chris, and I left Burlington the morning of December 23 to drive back to Virginia. My parents were torn. We all wanted to stay, but we also wanted to celebrate Christmas together – and not in a hospital. The family gifts were in Roanoke. There was nothing else we could do for Grandma in Vermont. We had said our goodbyes, so my parents decided it was okay to leave. Chris and I drove back with my parents, followed by Heather, Adam, Alex, and Travis in another car.

Later that night, as we were driving on the interstate through Pennsylvania, Aunt Eileen called Mom to tell her that Grandma had passed. "She's with the angels now," Eileen said. As I felt the tears running down my face, I took comfort knowing Grandma was finally at peace. The rest of the ride home was very quiet.

> *O Divine Master grant that I may not so much*
> *Seek to be consoled as to console;*
> *To be understood, as to understand;*
> *To be loved, as to love. For it is in*
> *Giving that we receive, it is in*
> *Pardoning that we are pardoned.*
> *And it is in dying that we are born to eternal life.*

- Prayer of Saint Francis

◊◊◊

Christmas Eve in Roanoke was a disaster. I slept most of the day, because my head was still pounding. Our schedule was the same as it had been every year since we were kids: Go to Christmas Eve mass, come home, change into the new pajamas my parents bought for all of us, and then wake up on Christmas morning and open presents.

We went to mass at a local Catholic church. My mom hated this church, but as they say it was the only show in town. She and my dad had moved to Roanoke in 1998. They loved the area, but Catholics didn't have as many options in Virginia as they did in Vermont. Mom missed Holy Cross Church, where she and Grandma went. We arrived at the church about forty-five minutes before mass. The choir was singing Christmas hymns – many of Grandma's favorites – and Mom lost it. She was really angry about Grandma's passing. She felt the doctors should have found the cancer earlier, when it was still treatable. She was feeling guilty for not paying more attention to Grandma's complaints about stomach pains when they spoke on the phone. And she was feeling even more guilt about not being there when her mom died. She started crying, and said she had to leave. Dad, Mom, Chris, and I went out to the car. Heather, Adam, and Travis stayed for the mass. We waited for them in the parking lot, and then drove home.

By the time we got back to the house, we were all exhausted, emotionally and physically. Tomorrow would be better. It would be Christmas Day.

◊◊◊

I woke up Christmas morning feeling even worse than the day before. We exchanged our gifts. Chris gave me a locket that had a place for a picture of our new baby. My headache had returned in force, so I went back to bed for a few hours after we opened presents.

We had an early dinner because Adam had to catch a flight back to Atlanta. Heather and Alex were planning to stay another week. After dinner, I was at the sink doing dishes. Adam's bags were packed and Dad and Travis were getting ready to take him to the airport.

My head was pounding. I turned around to say goodbye to Adam and fell to the floor, on my hands and knees. I started crying, because I didn't know what was happening. I was having a horrible time with my words.

Chris was upstairs, and Mom screamed for him. He ran downstairs, got down on the floor with me, and asked me if I was okay. "I don't know," I said, barely able to get the words out. He and Dad decided to take me to the emergency room. I just wanted my head to stop hurting – and my baby to be safe.

Chapter 6

Three Months

Dad was a vice president at Carilion, which owned Roanoke Memorial Hospital, so during the ride to the emergency room he was his cell phone, calling his contacts. Even though it was Christmas night, he made sure there was a full team waiting for us when we arrived. They took me right in.

The ER doctor and an OB/GYN who was on call did a series of tests on both me and the baby, which all came back negative. The ER doctor then recommended a CT scan. They brought me down to radiology, hooked me up, and began taking pictures of my brain. Chris was in the adjacent room with the technician as the images popped up on the screen. He noticed something strange: a large, dark red spot on the right side of the screen – the left side of my brain. Chris pointed toward the spot and asked, "What is *that*?"

"I don't know," the technician responded. "I'm just operating the machine. The doctor will look at the scan and then come talk to you."

Chris knew something was wrong. The nurse brought me back to the ER room, and Chris began to get very emotional. I was still struggling with my speech. It was almost like I had a mini-stroke.

Chris left to talk with Dad, and the OB/GYN came in to tell me what was going on. "It looks like you have a very large tumor in your brain," she told me, describing the baseball-sized mass that the scan showed in the lower left lobe. "We need to think about how we're going to treat it, because we need to address this right away." She was very frank, saying that most of these types of tumors were terminal. She added that a neurosurgeon was on his way to speak with us about next steps.

I was stunned. All I could think was, *What the fuck? Why are they telling me this? They must be wrong!*

While the OB/GYN doctor was talking to me, the ER doctor was giving the news to Chris and Dad in the hallway. Chris then came into my room, sat in a chair beside the bed, put his head on my stomach, and began crying. Dad walked in, stood to my left, took my hand, and kissed my forehead. He was crying, too. "We will figure this out," he said. Watching the two strongest men in my life in tears, I started crying with them.

A few minutes later, the neurosurgeon came in. He was, to put it bluntly, an asshole. He got right to the point: "Tracey, you have a glioblastoma." It was the first time I'd heard that word, which I soon learned described an extremely aggressive form of brain cancer. "If we take the tumor out tomorrow, I can probably get you three months to live if you keep the baby. If you abort the baby you would have approximately six months to live. This is serious, and I'm very sorry."

Sorry? Really? What kind of doctor comes into the ER and tells you that you have no choice but to die? And that your baby also has to die? I had finally reached a point where I'd never been happier with work, my husband, my pregnancy, and my body. I was thirty years old and thrilled with every aspect of my life. And now someone was sitting here telling me that I was going to die? With a baby inside me? I just could not comprehend what I'd been told. I refused to believe it. I just stared at him.

Chris broke the awkward silence. "I don't like your outcome, so you're not going to touch her," he said. "We're going back to

Houston." Houston was not just our home – it was also home to the MD Anderson Cancer Center, one of the most respected cancer facilities in the world. Dad took Chris to a conference room where he called a friend from business school, Todd Caliva, who worked at The Woman's Hospital of Texas. "I need the best brain surgeon in Houston," Chris pleaded. Todd called him back a few minutes later to tell him that Dr. Raymond Sawaya, the head of the neurosurgery department at MD Anderson, would meet with us as soon as we returned to Houston. I'm still amazed when I think that all of this happened on Christmas night.

They kept me in the hospital overnight. As a nurse was moving me to a private room in the maternity ward, Chris was frantically trying to find us a flight back to Houston the next day. Dad drove back to the house to tell Mom, Heather, and Travis in person – he tried calling from the hospital but couldn't say the words over the phone.

When Dad returned home and told the family the news, Mom lost it. She started throwing things, and screaming, and swearing at God. This woman had received plenty of bad news over the years, beginning in 1967 when she learned that Dad, then her fiancé, had been shot in Vietnam while serving in the Green Berets. But learning that her firstborn child had terminal brain cancer was the worst moment of her life.

Mom called a friend from work and asked her to come over and stay with Alexandra so the rest of the family could return to the hospital. Even though it was 9 p.m. on Christmas night, her friend came right over. Back at the hospital, Heather and Travis sat with me for a while, cracking jokes and making me laugh. Then Chris came in to tell me he'd managed to get us a flight back to Houston the next day.

The nurse on duty in the maternity ward was wonderful. She stayed with me all night, and we talked about everything and anything – although she did most of the talking, because I was still having trouble with my speech. And then she did something incredible: She asked if Chris and I wanted an ultrasound to see the baby. It was the first positive thing I'd heard since arriving at the emergency room.

The nurse lubed up my belly, put the transducer on it, and a few seconds later Chris and I, for the first time, saw our beautiful baby, seventeen weeks into the pregnancy. Both of our moods instantly changed – we were thrilled. Then the nurse asked if we wanted to know whether we were having a boy or a girl. We excitedly said yes. That's when we learned we were having a boy. We decided on a name: Raymond Jeffrey, in honor of Chris's dad, Raymond Schoettelkotte, and my dad, William Jeffrey Hilton. (Later, we would decide to call him by his middle name.) It felt great to focus on something positive, if only for a moment.

It was at that moment that I made a commitment to myself and my son: There is no way I'm going to die in three months. I will at the very least live until this child is born. I prayed and prayed, and then prayed some more, for that to happen.

◊◊◊

The next morning, December 26, we checked out of the hospital and went back to Mom and Dad's house to pack for our flight back to Houston. Chris had confirmed the appointment with Dr. Sawaya at MD Anderson for the following day. I gave Heather a list of friends to call about my situation. As I finished packing, I looked out the bedroom window and saw Chris and Dad talking below in the driveway. I could tell that Chris was crying. When they came in the house, both of them were in tears.

I asked to speak with Chris alone, and we went upstairs to the bedroom. I sat on the bed and looked at him.

"I cannot fight this fight on my own," I said. "I need you to buck up and fight this fight with me." It took all my strength just to get the words out, but I continued. "I can't deal with you or my father crying while I'm trying to fight this. I can't help you right now. I can't focus on you and your fears while we're going through this. I need you to walk the walk with me. I need you to be there for me." He looked at me, wiped away his tears, and gave me a huge hug. He got the message.

After we arrived at the airport, a new wave of reality set in, and then it was my turn to cry. I was terrified of what lay ahead.

Chapter 7

'Ready to Fight?'

The University of Texas MD Anderson Cancer Center is one of the world's most respected centers for cancer care, prevention, and research. Founded in 1941, the center is named after one of its main benefactors, Monroe Dunaway Anderson, who made his fortune in the early 1900s as a partner with the world's largest cotton merchant. MD Anderson employs nearly twenty thousand people and has served close to a million patients in its seventy-plus years of existence. The center has been ranked as one of the top two cancer centers in *U.S. News & World Report's* "Best Hospitals" survey each year since the survey began in 1990. Its facilities are just south of downtown Houston and cover more than fourteen million square feet, making it the world's largest freestanding cancer center.

I walked through the doors of MD Anderson for the first time on December 27, 2002, to meet with Dr. Raymond Sawaya, the director of MD Anderson's Brain and Spine Center and the chairman of the center's Department of Neurosurgery. We quickly realized that Chris's friend Todd was right: Dr. Sawaya was the best of the best, known for his pioneering work in brain tumor surgery, including less-invasive techniques designed to preserve as much of the "good" brain as possible during surgery to remove cancerous tumors.

After checking in, we were led to a conference room in MD Anderson's Brain and Spine Center. Mom and Dad were flying into Houston from Roanoke that morning. Chris's brother, Todd, and Todd's wife, Mignon, picked them up at the airport and drove them straight to MD Anderson. Chris and I wanted my parents to be with us for the meeting, and Dr. Sawaya and his physician's assistant, Michelle Hammond, were kind enough to wait for them.

After my parents arrived, Dr. Sawaya came into the conference room and sat down next to me. Chris gave Michelle the results of the CT scan from Roanoke and we started sharing the details of our trip to the emergency room on Christmas day – including the prognosis from "Dr. Jackass" that I had three months to live.

Dr. Sawaya took in all the information without saying much. He asked a few general questions about me and my pregnancy, and then began a few simple cognitive tests. He'd point to an object and ask me to say the word associated with that object. I was still struggling mightily with my speech at that point. When I couldn't say "wedding ring," I started crying. Chris – not the most patient of men – was getting upset and finally blurted out, "You've got to save my wife!" The inference was that saving me was more important than saving our baby.

Dr. Sawaya turned to me, put his hand on my knee, and looked me straight in the eye. "Tracey," he said, "before we talk about any of that, let's see what we can do to get this tumor out of you. Are you ready to fight the fight?" It was the question I had been longing for, and this time finding the right word was easy: "Yes!" I answered, repeating it for emphasis. Finally, here was someone who understood that all I wanted was a chance for my son to be born. Dr. Sawaya had learned from years of treating brain cancer patients that a positive mind-set is a critical part of the process. I needed to know that he would not abandon me, and that he and his team would do everything they could to help me. All I wanted was hope, and in that instant he gave it to me. I will love that man forever.

◊◊◊

Our meeting lasted for more than three hours, with Dr. Sawaya walking us through the diagnosis and the next steps. The surgery would be complex. I had a primary brain tumor, which is a less common form of cancer in general and brain tumors specifically. Only about forty thousand primary brain tumors are diagnosed in the United States annually, and a little less than half of those are benign. I had a highly malignant form called glioblastoma multiforme.

The location of the glioblastoma made things even more complicated. In the majority of people, including all right-handed people, the language centers are on the left side of the brain and usually in the temporal lobe – the precise location of my baseball-size tumor. That's why I was having trouble speaking and remembering words. As brain tumors grow, they can cause spontaneous bleeding, which is what triggered my persistent headaches and, ultimately, my collapse on Christmas day.

The other challenge, of course, was my pregnancy. Anesthesia would introduce risks to the baby, including the possibility of inducing premature labor. Dr. Sawaya brought in the anesthesiologist, Dr. David Ferson, to meet us and explain the process. Both doctors patiently answered all of our questions about the procedure and the risks.

Dr. Sawaya scheduled surgery for January 7. He wanted to have his "A team" of oncologists, radiologists, and others on board, and most of them were on vacation through the New Year. In the meantime, Dr. Swaim, my OB/GYN, had referred me to a new baby doctor named Joan Mastrobattista. Dr. Mastrobattista was a high-risk pregnancies specialist who would monitor me closely through the rest of my pregnancy.

Following our meeting with Dr. Sawaya, my condition quickly worsened. As each day passed, I had more trouble speaking. On

December 30, during my first visit with Dr. Mastrobattista, I couldn't answer her most basic questions: "What is your name?" "How old are you?" I began to cry. Dr. Mastro, as we called her, took Chris aside and said that she was going to call Dr. Sawaya and recommend moving up the surgery. She felt it needed to be performed as soon as possible. We ended up going straight from that appointment to MD Anderson to meet with Dr. Sawaya, who rescheduled the surgery for the next day, December 31. It was not the way I had envisioned ringing in the New Year. But if we had waited, I probably wouldn't have made it to 2003.

Chapter 8

Supercalifragilistic

My surgery was rescheduled for December 31, 2002, at 2 p.m., on the fifth floor of the University of Texas MD Anderson Cancer Center's Department of Neurosurgery. I arrived in the morning because Dr. Sawaya wanted an up-to-date MRI before the surgery. I was scared, because I knew I was dying. Physically, I was shot. I had no color in my face – my skin was gray. I was barely able to speak.

Sitting with Heather in the waiting room before the MRI, I struggled to tell her something that was very important to me. It took me a long time to get the words out.

"I don't know if I'm going to make it through this surgery," I finally said. "If I don't, I want to be kept alive until Jeffrey is old enough to be born." Heather and I had our ups and downs, as many sisters do, but I knew only she would understand what I was asking. Only she would make sure my dying wish was granted. Heather was one of my angels who would help me get through the day.

After the MRI, a nurse took me to pre-op. There was a lot of activity. The nurses measured my head. Dr. Ferson, the anesthesiologist, measured my head a second time, and then taped tiny sensors all over me – round, green foam stickers that would help the medical team monitor my various functions and vital signs during the surgery.

I kept thinking, *Why am I here?* I was thirty years old with a tumor in my brain. And then I looked to my right and saw a young girl, laying in a surgical bed just a few feet from me, also preparing for surgery. *We're both too young for this*, I thought. I don't know her outcome, but to this day I pray that she survived.

Mom, Heather, and Chris stayed with me in pre-op until the surgical nurse came in and said it was time. The three of them each gave me a kiss and said, "I love you." The nurse wheeled me from pre-op into the operating room. What a busy place! There seemed to be about 20 people in the operating room. An amazing group, led by Dr. Sawaya.

I was given a sedative to make me drowsy. The surgical staff positioned me on my right side. They wanted my head in a lateral position because the tumor was behind my left ear. I had padding under my knees and chest, so I was fairly comfortable. I could wiggle my toes when they needed me to, and move other parts of my body. Because the surgery is so long, Dr. Sawaya wants his patients to be able to stretch to stay as comfortable as possible. My head, however, was completely immobilized. A clamp with pins on both sides kept me from moving it at all, for obvious reasons.

My pregnancy did complicate preparations a bit. Anesthesia is only a risk to the fetus during the first trimester, and I was four and a half months along. But the doctors were still concerned that the anesthesia, if administered too quickly, could induce labor. Dr. Sawaya had asked Dr. Ferson to find a way to deliver the anesthesia more slowly than normal, which Dr. Ferson did beautifully. Beyond that, however, they didn't have to take any extra precautions to protect my son during the surgery.

The doctors really didn't know what type of cancer I had until they opened up my head. The MRI gave them some idea, but they didn't actually confirm that it was a glioblastoma until they saw it first-hand. What they did know was that it was a large mass –

around two-and-a-half inches in diameter – in the dominant hemisphere of my temporal lobe.

The cerebral cortex is the largest part of the human brain, and consists of four sections. The frontal lobe, located in the front left side of the brain, is in charge of recognizing things that happen and controls how we react to and deal with those things, through reasoning and problem solving. The frontal lobe also houses long-term memory functions. The parietal lobe, located behind the frontal lobe on the right side of the brain, processes sensory information such as touch, temperature, or taste. The occipital lobe, behind the parietal lobe, is associated with visual processing. The temporal lobe, on the lower left side of the brain, is responsible for short-term memory, comprehension, and speaking, writing, and reading functions. That's where my cancer was located, which is why I was having so much trouble speaking.

My tumor was "heterogeneous," meaning it was a mishmash of blood, solid mass, and fluid-filled cysts. Because of its size, it was putting quite a bit of pressure on my brain. Dr. Sawaya explained to us beforehand that because of the type of tumor and its location, he was unsure exactly how much of the cancer he would be able to remove. The goal, of course, is to extract as much of the mass as possible, but sometimes it's impossible to do without damaging important brain functions. This led to the most interesting part of the surgery: Dr. Sawaya and his team planned to wake me during the critical parts of the operation to test my cognitive functions. He credits Dr. Ferson with the idea of performing the "awake craniotomy." Dr. Sawaya said he had quite a bit of experience with this procedure, so we felt comfortable agreeing to it.

I was first sedated intravenously. The team then put a mask on me to give them more control over the anesthesia that would follow. The next step was a "scalp block" to completely numb my scalp. I was asleep for the first part of the operation – the part when they sawed my head open. (I was fine with not having to listen to all of the drilling and cutting!) Dr. Sawaya and his team used a variety of ultrasound and navigation tools to make their way to the tumor. Cutting through the skin, bone, and brain covering – called the *dura mater* – does not put any brain functions at risk. But when you get to the tumor, you can't just start chopping it out. The surgeons must make sure they don't disturb any speech, motor, or sensory areas. Language centers are different for everyone – their position changes from person to person, so the surgeon has to locate them during the procedure. Or at least rule out that they're in the way of his path to the tumor.

The goal with these types of surgeries is to find the border of the main mass of the tumor. Once Dr. Sawaya found the edge of the "wall" – he calls it a "pseudo-wall" because it's technically not a wall – he began making his way around the outer surface. If he encountered any functions, he would have to find another route.

"The key is not to find any language function that is in our way," Dr. Sawaya explained after the surgery. "If we do, then we have to go around that area and find another way to get into the tumor." In my case, the tumor mass was so large that it had pushed aside my speech function and language centers. This actually turned out to be a good thing, because it cleared the way for Dr. Sawaya to begin removing the tumor without risking any damage to my speech center or other functions.

Dr. Sawaya discovered that I actually had three interconnected tumors stacked on top of one another. He said it was amazing that I was functioning as well as I was with a mass of this size in my brain.

Once they reached the tumors, the team coagulated the areas where the tiny vessels are, and Dr. Sawaya then cut all the way around the surface of the mass. There was more good news: the large cyst at the core was filled with fluid as opposed to being a solid mass. Once Dr. Sawaya drained the fluid, he had a lot more room in which to work. He was able to dissect the full 360 degrees of the tumor, which enabled him to remove the entire mass.

After the brain was exposed, Dr. Sawaya asked Dr. Ferson to wake me up so he could run some tests. He wanted to make sure the steps he was taking to remove the tumor weren't affecting key speech or memory functions. There was an important side benefit to this approach: Waking me up meant they would administer much less anesthesia, which further reduced the risk to the baby.

I woke up fairly quickly after Dr. Ferson reduced the anesthesia. I could hear the surgical team talking, and then I opened my eyes. The first person I saw was Dr. Ferson. He started with some simple tests – asking me to identify objects in pictures, followed by some counting, to make sure that I was awake and alert. Next, the team began low-level stimulation, using electrical current on the parts of the brain adjacent to the tumor, a procedure called brain mapping or cortical mapping. They didn't need to find the speech center – they just had to determine that it wasn't in the way. As long as they didn't encounter any functions, they could continue with the extraction of the tumor.

Next came an unexpected question from Dr. Sawaya: "Are you ready to call your husband?" I was shocked, but quickly answered, "Yes!" Someone called the waiting room. Several family members, friends, and co-workers had gathered there for the long wait. Chris, Mom and Dad, Heather, and Travis were there. Todd and Mignon were there. One of the partners at Beck Redden, Alistair Dawson, and his wife Wendy were there as well.

Wendy had given me a beautiful angel the day before the surgery. The angel still sits above the front door of my house. Everyone in the room had given up their New Year's Eve to support me through what would be a seven-hour surgery. It was probably worse for them than it was for me. They just had to sit and wait.

And then the phone rang. Dr. Ferson asked for Chris, and when Chris came on he put the phone to my ear. Chris was expecting to hear Dr. Sawaya's voice – but instead he heard mine. "Honey, I'm okay," I said. It was a quick call. We each said, "I love you," and that was it.

Dr. Sawaya continued his testing after the call, and I continued talking. At one point, I felt a sharp pain. "I don't know what you're doing," I told him, "but that one hurt!" So they upped the anesthesia a bit. We joked about New Year's Eve. "Don't you all have spouses that you should be taking out to dinner?" I asked at one point. I later told Dr. Sawaya that I'd give him a bottle of Cristal to share with his wife for their *next* New Year's Eve. (It took me three years, but I finally delivered the gift.)

Before they put me back under, Dr. Sawaya asked if I wanted to call Chris again. This time, Chris was a little more relaxed. He jokingly asked, "Can you say 'supercalifragilistic'?" I said, "No, but I can say 'supercalifragilisticexpialidocious!" He laughed and said to the others in the room, "Tracey just said 'supercalifragilistic-expialidocious'." They all cheered. I said goodbye, and Dr. Ferson put me back under for the rest of the surgery.

Once the extraction was complete, the team did one last pass with the ultrasound to make sure no pieces of the tumor were hiding. There was no bleeding, so they closed up my head, layer by layer.

Dr. Sawaya described the procedure as fairly routine – as routine as removing a large glioblastoma can be, I guess. After the surgery he went to the waiting room to tell my family that the surgery was a success.

I woke up in the ICU an hour later. The nurses and doctors were gathered at the end of the bed. Someone asked, "How are you feeling?" I answered softly: "I'm still here."

Chapter 9

Switching Places

The first time I opened my eyes in the ICU, I had no idea where I was. The first person I saw was Dr. Ferson, my anesthesiologist. Standing next to Dr. Ferson was a nurse – a really large African-American man who looked just like Michael Clark Duncan in *The Green Mile*. My head was bandaged in a big balloon of white gauze. I was heavily medicated. I couldn't move. I couldn't speak. I remember feeling grumpy – very grumpy!

Dr. Ferson explained where I was and recounted the surgery that I'd just been through. Shortly thereafter, Dr. Sawaya came in. "You did a really good job," he told me, adding that he was very happy with the outcome of the surgery. A few minutes later, Chris came in, smiling and a little scared – he wasn't sure what to expect. He asked how I was doing and made other small talk, but all I could do was look at him because I still couldn't speak. I wondered silently, *How come I was able to speak during the surgery, but now I can't?* I wanted so badly to tell Chris that I had made it through and I was doing okay. But all I could do was look at him – which in itself was a great feeling.

Chris asked the nurse if the rest of the family could come in. "Just for a few seconds," he said. One by one, they came into my line of sight – Mom, Dad, Heather, and Travis. I don't remember what they said, but I do recall lots of smiles and many tears. Everyone was tired and hungry after spending the day in the waiting room, so after a few minutes they left to get something to eat. It was late in the evening on New Year's Eve, soon to be 2003. What a Happy New Year for us all!

The doctors left shortly after my family. The nurse dosed me up to go to sleep, even though he would be waking me up every hour throughout the night to check on me. I can't remember his name, and my family says he was a great guy – but every time he woke me, I was not his greatest fan. All I wanted was to sleep. I'm sure I grunted at him a couple of times to voice my displeasure.

The night soon got interesting. I felt a presence near the bed. Opening my eyes, I saw Grandma sitting above me! She was in a spot where I could see her without turning my head, and she looked gorgeous and happy – happier than I'd seen her in a long time. Her white hair – she had stopped coloring it after her car accident – was glimmering. She had on a pretty ivory dress that matched her hair perfectly. *I must be dreaming,* I thought. *Either that, or I'm losing my mind!*

After a moment, Grandma spoke. I could hear her voice in my head, clear as day. *"How are you feeling, Tracey?"* she asked.

"I think I'm doing all right," I answered, without speaking. She could hear my thoughts. *"What are you doing here, Grandma?"*

"I wanted to check on you."

"Why did you leave us so suddenly?" I asked.

"Well, I knew something was wrong with you – that you were very sick," Grandma responded. *"I also knew it was not your time. You had a baby in your tummy. So I switched with you."*

I looked at her quizzically. *"What do you mean, you switched with me?"*

Her big blue eyes widened. *"I'm here with my sister now, and you're going to stay at home with your family,"* she said. Grandma's sister, Virginia, had died in 1980. *"It's going to be okay,"* she added. *"Go back to sleep."*

I drifted back into unconsciousness.

◊◊◊

Later that night, Grandma returned, and this time she had company. Chris's dad, Ray, who had passed away four years earlier, and Chris's older brother, Jeff, who had died before Chris was born, were both there with Grandma. Jeff seemed to be in his twenties or thirties now – but he never spoke. He stood silently next to his father, and I remember thinking, *You're much shorter than your brothers!* Chris is six-foot-five and his younger brother Todd is six-foot-nine. Ray was six-foot-three and Jeff, standing next to him, looked to be several inches shorter. I thought, *How did Jeff miss out on those Schoettelkotte tall genes?*

I had met Ray a half-dozen times before he suffered the stroke that killed him on August 31, 1998. That man made me feel like I was the sun, the moon, and the stars! Raymond Joseph Schoettelkotte, Jr., was born on March 10, 1943, the son of Raymond Joseph Sr. and Ada Baechle Schoettelkotte. He had two older sisters, Elizabeth (Betty) and Margaret (Margie), and two younger siblings: sister Jeanie and brother James (Jim). Ray Jr. grew up in Lawrenceville, Indiana, the great-grandson of German immigrants who had fled Germany into the Netherlands as the first German Empire was rising.

When Ray Sr. was old enough, he and his brother John bought the town's General Store from John's father-in-law, John Raehm. The Schoettelkotte Brothers General Store was founded in 1927, and it could have been a model for Oleson's Mercantile in "Little House on the Prairie." The brothers Schoettelkotte sold everything from barbed wire to animal feed to food and clothing.

The store also housed the local U.S. Post Office for Lawrenceville. During Prohibition, Ray also did a bit of moonshining out of the basement – even using the grapes that grew in the field next to the store for winemaking. Rumor has it that John Dillinger – Public Enemy No. 1 – stopped by on occasion to buy sugar corn and sample Ray's hooch.

Eleven years after Ray bought the store, he married Ada, a pretty lady who brought eggs from her family's farm to sell at the store. Fifty-five years later, Ray Jr. bought the general store from his father while working at a company called FMC. He had started college in the fall of 1961 at Indiana Central University. Ray and his first wife Margaret Burst (Margo) had three sons: Jeff, Chris, and Todd. Jeff died in 1967 at the age of two because of a hole in his heart – a horrible loss for Margo and Ray. A year later, in May of 1968, Chris was born, followed by Todd in November of 1970.

Ray and Margo divorced in 1978, and several years later Ray married the woman he said was the love of his life: Pamela Wood. I first met Ray and Pam in 1997, when Chris graduated from the University of Houston with his masters degree in business.

Ray had a presence about him. When Chris and I visited him in the hospital following his stroke in 1998, Ray gave me flowers that someone had sent to him and told Chris and I that he wanted to see us get married right then and there! We left the hospital that night and drove to a local hotel. Before we even got the bags out of the car we received a call telling us to head back to the hospital immediately. Ray passed away shortly after we arrived, leaving us all in a state of shock.

◊◊◊

Seeing Ray and Jeff by my bedside the first night after my surgery was less of a shock only because I had already seen – and spoken with – Grandma. But it was odd to see them with Grandma, since she and Ray had never met. At one point the two of them were talking about something that I couldn't follow. Then the party got even bigger, as Papa O'Regan and Grampy Hilton joined the group. It was a crowded room indeed! Grandma was trying to tell me something, and Papa interrupted her. He was telling me to come join them. Grandma turned to Papa, put her arms across her chest, and told him very sternly, *"Be quiet!"* She had waited a long time to do that. I smiled and said to myself, *Heaven must be a really good place.*

Grampy Hilton was an old-timer from South Portland, Maine. He worked for a canvas manufacturer called Leavitt & Parris for more than thirty-five years, building sails and covers for boats and awnings for businesses. Grampy and his wife Winnie made a great couple and had five children: four boys, including my dad Bill, the oldest, along with Bill's brothers Phil, Howie, and David, and one daughter, Deb. The boys all worked with their father each summer. One day when my dad was fifteen or sixteen, he was with Grampy delivering sails to the owner of a large sailboat. Grampy noticed the guide wire on the starboard side of the boat had become unattached, so he volunteered my father to go up to the top of the mast and re-bolt the wire. It was windy that day, and after Grampy and the boat's owner winched Dad to the top of the mast, he was swaying six feet to the starboard and six feet to port, making the task very difficult indeed. Dad says that's the reason he owns a powerboat instead of a sailboat.

Grampy Hilton also asked me to join the rest of them in heaven, but Grandma quickly shut him down too. *"No, she's not coming with us,"* she said.

Ray agreed: *"Tracey, your grandmother is right."*

"I can't do that right now, Grampy," I said silently, as my eyes met his, hoping he would understand why.

"Do me a favor then," he said. *"Tell your father we have the cribbage board ready and we're waiting for him up here."* Cribbage, Old Milwaukee, lobsters, and my Grammy Hilton were his favorite things in life.

Seeing all of these deceased relatives left me confused, but I was very certain about what I saw. I took comfort knowing that they were all ready to welcome me in heaven.

◇◇◇

Several weeks later, Father Roger Charbonneau, the pastor at Holy Cross Church, which I attended while growing up in Colchester, shared a story with Aunt Eileen and Uncle Brian as they were cleaning out Grandma's apartment at the senior housing complex behind the church. Father Charbonneau and Grandma were very close, and he had administered her last rites in the hospital. On December 22, the day before she passed, she told him a story.

"We need to pray for Tracey. She's sick," she told Father Charbonneau. This was three days before I collapsed in the kitchen of my parents' house in Virginia. My cancer had not yet been diagnosed. "I need to go now. I need to take her place." Together, they prayed for me. The next night, Grandma died peacefully.

"Theresa had great confidence in the power of prayer," Father Charbonneau told us later. "She really believed something would happen for Tracey, and she was dedicated to making that happen – even if it meant offering her own sufferings for the sake of Tracey's healing."

Chapter 10

I See Dead People

Relatives – living and dead – weren't the only people I saw during my first night in the intensive care unit. Lying in my bed, I could look out into the hallway. It was a busy place. There were doctors, nurses – and more dead people. I didn't know any of them, but I knew they weren't alive. They were grayish in color, and translucent. They would walk through – not around – the hospital personnel. The staff didn't seem to be paying attention to them – probably because they couldn't see them or feel their presence.

I didn't know who they were, but it was clear they were people who had passed on but hadn't left the physical earth. They were just walking, wandering in different directions, with no real purpose. It was like they didn't know what they were supposed to do next.

I remember two people distinctly. One woman was skinny, and not very tall. She had white hair. Another, a man, was in his fifties or sixties. Both were wearing pajamas. Neither said anything as they walked past my room.

As I watched them, I couldn't help but think: *I'm going fucking crazy*. And then I drifted off to sleep.

In the morning – New Year's Day – a different nurse came in. She was an older woman and she was very curt. "Sit up," she commanded. I tried, but it was very painful. Everything hurt. She finally got me to sit up in bed. Victory! And then she demanded that I stand up. That was even worse, but with her help I did it. She moved me to a chair near the bed. My head was still covered in gauze. The doctors had started me on steroids, which reduced the probability of having a seizure. But the steroids made my face bloated and puffy. I felt terrible.

I was sitting in the chair when Chris came in. He still wasn't sure what to expect or how to act. He didn't know whether he could kiss me. I could tell he was very nervous about being with me. No one tells the caregivers what to do or what to expect the day after a loved one's brain surgery. It's easy to be overwhelmed by the fear of what comes next, and I'm sure that's what Chris was feeling.

He was dressed like I remembered him on our first date: dark blue jeans, a white button-down shirt, and black cowboy boots. He said hi, but I still couldn't speak. He sat and stayed with me for the rest of the day and into the night.

Dr. Sawaya came by in the morning to check on me. He removed the gauze to get a look at his handiwork. Before my surgery, one of the nurses had braided my hair on the part of my head that they didn't have to shave. The braid was caked in dried blood. Dr. Sawaya examined the staples he used to close the incision. They formed a sideways "C," starting about two inches from the back of my left ear and curling underneath toward the front of the ear. He said everything looked great, and left.

Later in the day (I couldn't say when exactly, since I had no sense of time), the nurses moved me from the chair to a wheelchair – the first step in moving me out of the ICU and into a different recovery room.

On January 2, I was moved into a private room and had a steady stream of visitors throughout the day. In the afternoon, Chris, Dad, Travis, and Todd took a break from my bedside to go to the Rice University men's basketball game. I encouraged them with a wave of my hand to go – they needed a break. Todd had played basketball at Rice a few years earlier, so when they came back they brought me a basketball signed by the entire team, wishing me well.

My speech started to come back later that day, but it was still difficult. I could say "yes" and "no," but not much else. I couldn't say anyone's name or let anyone know how I was feeling. I certainly could not begin to tell them about Grandma and Ray and the others I'd spoken with the night before.

After the Rice game, Chris returned to the hospital and stayed with me overnight. The private room was bigger than my room in the ICU, but the small reclining chair next to the bed was no match for his size. He tried sleeping in it, but it was much too small for his large frame.

My night was even more restless than his, however. At one point, I felt a disturbance in the darkness. I opened my eyes and saw one of the most terrifying sights I've ever seen. Black ghosts filled the room. They were flying back and forth, zooming past my head. They were trying to get me to go with them. I screamed – silently – and grabbed for Chris's arm. *I don't want to go! I want to stay! Don't make me go!* I yelled, without saying a word. Chris knew I was terrified – my eyes told the story – but I couldn't tell him what I was seeing. I gripped Chris's hand and held on for dear life. Eventually – it seemed like forever – the flying ghosts left, and never came back.

That episode was enough for Chris; he was very disturbed and didn't want to spend another night with me in that room. I couldn't blame him – I wasn't very good company. Mom spent the next two nights with me, sleeping in the chair.

The second day in recovery, Mom took me by wheelchair down to a hair salon in the hospital, one designed especially for cancer patients. The hair stylist rinsed a lot of the blood out of my hair and Mom and I looked at a variety of hats, scarves, and wigs – the accessories women wear when they lose their hair during chemotherapy. We didn't buy anything.

Dr. Sawaya had scheduled an MRI to make sure everything looked good after the surgery. He was pleased to show us that all of the tumors had been removed. I was still having trouble speaking at that point, although that was expected. My speech improved slowly as the days progressed. But it was a lot of work for me; it was an early sign that my ability to find words would be a challenge going forward. They just weren't stored in the same places they used to be.

Grandma visited that night again – briefly – to remind me that everything would be all right. It was very comforting to see her. That third night in the hospital was when my body really started to feel the effects of the surgery and recovery. Being kept still on my right side for seven hours of surgery did a number on my back and my right shoulder, and the pain would wake me throughout the night. Every time I woke up, Mom was there to gently massage my aching muscles until I fell back asleep.

When I awoke the next morning, a half-dozen white angels were gathered around me. They were sitting still, and all of them were smiling at me. They remained with me for the rest of my time in the hospital.

I had other visitors during my three days in the recovery room. My friend Vickie came by on the second day. When she entered the room, I could see the fear in her eyes. I must have looked horrible! She brought flowers. I tried to say thank you to her before she left. I couldn't really get the words out, but she understood.

A Baptist preacher who was making the rounds with patients came into my room and asked if I wanted to pray. Several visitors were there at the time – Mom, Heather, Pam, Mignon, Travis's girlfriend Mackenzie, and Danny, a neighbor of mine from Humble. We all held hands, prayed with the preacher, and said "Amen" when she was done. It was a nice reminder that everyone needed to continue praying.

Pam was a regular visitor, helping anyone who needed something to eat or drink. Heather was another regular, keeping Mom calm and doing lots of little things, like calling my friends to update them on my status. She was pregnant at the time, too, making her support all the more unbelievable.

On the fourth day, I met a woman named Karen Kemp. Karen's husband Michael also had brain cancer and his surgery was the same day as mine. His was in the morning, and mine was in the afternoon. Karen and Michael were both in their early fifties, and Karen and my mom ended up being very close friends. Michael was British and was the general manager of the Four Seasons Hotel in Thailand. His tumor was diagnosed in Bangkok at the highly regarded Bumrungrad Hospital. Karen was an Army brat who lived for many years in Germany. Michael and Karen had met overseas while they both were working for the Four Seasons. They dated for several years, which was a challenge because while one was in one time zone, the other was often halfway across the globe. They finally decided to get married, with Karen retiring while Michael managed the hotel in Thailand. They ended up in Houston after Michael's brain tumor was diagnosed.

Ironically, the Kemps would end up buying our house in Cypress. Chris and I had invited them over to dinner a year and a half after our surgeries. We were just getting ready to list our house and move into the model home we had bought in Humble and leased back to the builder. The lease was up and we were eager to move. Karen and Michael wanted to be closer to MD Anderson, so the Cypress house was a perfect location for them.

The fourth day was my last at the hospital. After a final round of tests, I was discharged, and the family took me home. Dad drove, and the rest of us – Mom, Chris, Heather, Pam, and I – packed into the Suburban. I was still out of it. I don't remember much about leaving, other than saying goodbye to the Kemps. I was glad to be going home.

Chapter 11

Living in Fear

My first few days at home were one big blur. Mom and Heather were planning to have a baby shower for me before Heather flew back to Atlanta the following week. I probably wasn't ready for a party, physically or mentally. I was still having a really hard time getting my words out, and I had about 30 staples in my head.

Before the baby shower, my scalp was itching like crazy. I asked Heather to look at the area around the incision – which was, in her words, "pretty raunchy." My hair and scalp were still caked with dried blood. Dr. Sawaya had told us that I couldn't wash my hair by myself for a few days. So Heather took me into the bathroom, undid my braid, and used rubbing alcohol to carefully remove the blood from my hair. Heather has done many things for me over the years, but this simple act was one of the kindest. Everyone was amazing throughout the whole ordeal, but Heather stood out, despite being pregnant – and puking a lot, as I recall. She was there for me day and night during that first week after surgery. A sister's love should never be forgotten – and I'll never forget what she did for me.

About twenty people came to the shower – family, friends, and neighbors – but to me it felt like a gazillion bodies were crammed into the house. I was so tired I could barely talk, so I'm sure I wasn't a good guest of honor. But the shower helped me to remember why I was still here: I had a baby inside me.

◊◊◊

The night before Heather left, a group of us was sitting at the kitchen table after dinner. Mom, Dad, Heather, Pam, Chris, and I were casually talking. My speech was coming back slowly but surely, though there were still certain words and phrases I couldn't say, like "wedding ring." But I did my best to tell the story of how Grandma visited me in the hospital after my surgery. Not surprisingly, they were skeptical. "What do you mean you were talking to Grandma?" someone asked.

I told them as much as I could remember: How Grandma came to my side and said she had switched places with me. How Chris's dad Ray and brother Jeff visited – and how Jeff was all grown up. How Grampy had promised to have the cribbage board ready for Dad. And how Grandma had told Papa to shut up! I told the story very matter-of-factly, and everyone seemed stunned. I don't think anyone truly believed what I was saying. They all *wanted* to believe my story, but for obvious reasons they couldn't get their heads around it. The conversation eventually turned to something else.

A few months later Chris asked me about seeing his brother, whom he had never met. We talked about Jeff and Chris's dad. Chris started to believe that maybe he would see his dad again someday, and that cheered us both up.

◊◊◊

The staples were in my scalp for a little over a week. Some fell out on their own; for the rest, I returned to MD Anderson, where a physician's assistant removed them. It was around that time that I met with the two specialists who would take over my treatment: Dr. Morris Groves, a neuro-oncologist who would be responsible for my chemotherapy and steroid treatments, and Dr. Stephen Hahn, a radiation oncologist who would oversee my radiation treatments. Dr. Groves was also a lawyer, so I felt a connection with him. Dr. Hahn was a no-nonsense kind of guy.

Dr. Groves decided the chemo treatments should wait until after I had the baby because the risk to the fetus would be too high. The radiation treatments, however, started just a few weeks after the surgery, once I regained some of my strength. The radiation had to start as quickly as possible to zap any remaining cancerous cells and prevent the tumors from growing back.

The treatments were scheduled for five weeks, five days a week, with the weekends off. Each treatment was around twenty minutes long, with the radiologist administering small portions of what doctors call a "50 gray" dose over the five weeks. I wasn't allowed to drive yet, so Mom stayed with me during the first few weeks of treatment, playing chauffeur on the hour-long drive from Cypress to downtown Houston in the early mornings. When Mom had to return home to Virginia, she set up a schedule with some of our neighbors to drive me to and from MD Anderson for my remaining treatments.

During the long early-morning drives, Mom and I talked a lot about how I was feeling. Mom was one of the few people who treated me as a survivor and not a victim. She never talked to me about dying. We shared the belief that I was going to make it – no ifs, ands, or buts.

Michael Kemp was also receiving radiation treatments during this time, and our paths often crossed at MD Anderson. Mom and Karen Kemp often sat together during our treatments, and they bonded during those times. I still can't have lunch with Karen without my mom joining us!

The radiation was very targeted. I wore special headgear – it looked like a colander – with three X's forming a border around the area where the glioblastoma had initially grown. The radiation was pinpointed on those three spots. The "helmet" had a facemask that was connected to a specially constructed, heavy steel plate that covered my neck and chest, all the way down to my abdomen, as I lay on my back. The shield, which was lowered from the ceiling, was designed to protect my unborn baby, who was only five months along when the treatments started. The doctors were confident; they estimated that just 0.0000015 percent of the radiation would reach the fetus – an amount that would keep my son healthy and growing. Even so, I was scheduled for weekly ultrasounds with Dr. Mastrobattista, the high-risk neonatal doctor who had taken over my care, to monitor the baby's development.

The worst part of the radiation treatments was how much they exhausted me. I threw up a lot, which also sucked. But they were also keeping me alive. I was bound and determined to live long enough to give birth to a healthy baby boy. I had the best physicians helping me, and they were just as determined as I was – partly because pulling this off would be a feather in their cap.

I lost most of my remaining hair during the radiation treatments. One patch remained on the very top of my head – very punk rockish. Chris said I looked like one of the natives from the Daniel Day Lewis movie, "The Last of the Mohicans."

I had put off buying a wig, but eventually decided to give it a try as my hair loss worsened. It seemed that every time I got out of the shower, I'd pull out another clump of hair. There was another reason I needed a self-esteem boost: To keep me strong, the doctors were pumping me with steroids and a 2,000-calorie-a-day diet, and my weight ballooned.

A year earlier, I looked better than I ever had before. Now I was a moose – 187 pounds, with a three-inch patch of hair on the top of my head. It was not the most glamorous time of my life. In addition, the steroids were giving me wild mood swings. It was a tough stretch for me emotionally. Chris finally convinced me that a wig would make me feel better about myself.

I started my search in the wig shop at MD Anderson – what's a cancer center without a wig shop? – but all the wigs there were too small for my head. After a couple of weeks of looking around at different shops, Chris, being Chris, took me to the most prestigious wig shop in all of Houston. By this point, I had decided on a blond wig. I had always wanted to be blond, so why not? Chris helped me pick out what turned out to be a very expensive wig, and waited while I was fitted. I hated the search and was glad it was over.

After leaving the wig shop, we went out to dinner at a nearby P.F. Chang's. As I was eating, Chris noticed that every time I took a bite, the wig would slide back on my head about a quarter of an inch. I was oblivious to what was happening. By the time the wig had slid back about three inches, Chris – who knew I was extremely self-conscious about wearing it – said in a very measured tone, "Tracey, every time you take a bite, your wig slips back on your head." I was mortified – and pissed. I reached up, grabbed the top of the wig, and yanked it forward. The move was very un-ladylike, but I didn't care what the other diners thought. This was the new me – someone who cared about being alive more than I cared about how I looked in public. We quickly finished our dinner, paid the tab, and left the restaurant. When we reached the car I pulled the wig off and threw it in the back seat. I never wore it again. It was probably the worst $700 we ever spent. From then on, until my hair grew back a few months later, I happily wore hats.

◊◊◊

Between the radiation, the steroids, and my concern for the baby, I was a physical and emotional wreck. My doctors and my family were worried about me. The oncology team wanted to start my chemo treatments as soon as possible, concerned that waiting would increase the chances of the cancer returning. But they had to wait until I gave birth. All I cared about was having a healthy child.

Dr. Mastrobattista's goal – which I wholeheartedly endorsed – was to keep the pregnancy going as long as the fetus was still growing inside me. Once she determined that he would begin to grow faster on his own, it would be time to have the baby.

I was around six months pregnant when the radiation ended, and I began to feel much better. And believe it or not, I was bored. Chris was back at work. Mom, Dad, Heather, Travis, and Pam had all gone home, back to their "regular" lives. So I decided to go back to my regular life as well. I had worked so hard to become a lawyer and desperately wanted to spend some time in the office. The partners at Beck Redden weren't sure what to make of me at that point – a pregnant, bald, and speech-challenged woman – so they gave me a lot of menial tasks, like writing summaries and reviewing documents. Some words remained elusive when I was speaking or writing, so I didn't mind the tedious work. It helped me get back into a routine.

The doctors kept close tabs on my progress. The weekly ultrasounds were great because they reassured Chris and me that our baby was developing properly – that all of his body parts were in the right places and growing. During one of the ultrasounds, Dr. Mastro mentioned that she could not see Jeffrey's feet. Chris thought the world was ending. I calmly told them both that I was sure he had two feet – because he was kicking me with them every day. Chris remained worried about those feet until I gave birth.

More worrisome was the fact that the ultrasounds couldn't tell us whether our son had any brain damage from my radiation treatments. There was a constant undercurrent of fear for the remainder of my pregnancy. But Grandma continued to give me comfort during this stressful time. She would visit me occasionally when I was resting. I couldn't see her, but I could feel her. *"Is everything going to be okay?"* I would ask. *"Is this going to work? Am I doing the right thing?"* Her response was always the same: *"Yes, Tracey, you're going to be fine."*

Jeffrey's growth inside me began to slow in early May, about thirty-six weeks into the pregnancy. Dr. Mastro decided it was time for me to have my baby.

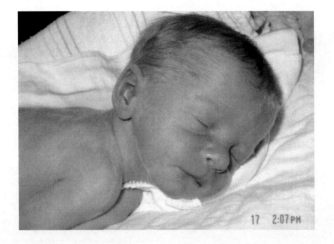

Chapter 12

4 Pounds, 9 Ounces

Dr. Mastrobattista scheduled the delivery for May 14, the thirty-sixth week of my pregnancy. I was admitted to a new neonatal care unit at Children's Memorial Hermann Hospital in Houston. We arrived at the hospital around 3 p.m., and after checking in the staff assigned me to a delivery room. Chris, Mom, and Pam sat with me in the smallish room, and together we waited for Dr. Mastro. It was the beginning of a long day and night. The medical team first put me on pitocin to induce labor. I started having contractions quickly but was not dilating. So we waited. And waited some more. Into the night I went, and then the next morning, with the contractions continuing, but no dilation. Twenty-five hours later, I was still at it. Finally, Dr. Mastrobattista determined that the contractions were starting to put stress on the baby, so she decided to do an immediate C-section.

Chris, wearing scrubs, stayed close behind as the medical staff wheeled me into the operating room. Dr. Mastrobattista worked quickly. The procedure took no more than five minutes. She made the incision on my stomach, opened me up, and scooped Jeffrey out. Little did they know that Chris had brought a camera into the room and snapped a picture just as our son came out!

Raymond Jeffrey Schoettelkotte was born May 15, 2003, at 5:35 p.m., weighing in at four pounds, nine ounces.

The doctors sternly told Chris to put the camera away. Jeffrey was having trouble breathing. Chris cut the umbilical cord and the nurses handed Jeff to him. Chris held him near me so I could give our son a small kiss before the nurse whisked him away to clear his airway. Chris and I both had tears in our eyes. And then we heard one of the greatest sounds ever: Our newborn son crying and screaming!

I wouldn't see Jeff again until the next day. A nurse brought him one floor up to the neonatal intensive care unit while Dr. Mastro stitched me up. I was in pretty tough shape at that point, having lost a lot of blood during the delivery. They put me on a morphine drip. Chris, Mom, and Pam visited with me for a while, and then went to see Jeff so I could get some rest. Resting in his NICU crib, our son was hooked up to oxygen and more sensors than you can imagine. But he was healthy.

As the epidural began to wear off, I started feeling incredible pain – far more intense than anything I had experienced in my head before or after my brain surgery. Despite the morphine drip, I started screaming, convinced that I was going to die. Grandma visited again with a simple message: *Relax*.

Mom heard me screaming from down the hall and went looking for a nurse. She found Chris instead and explained what was happening. Chris tracked down Dr. Mastro, who came to my room, assessed my pain, and ordered a switch from morphine to Demerol. After what seemed like an eternity, the Demerol kicked in, the pain subsided, and I finally calmed down.

By the next morning, I was desperate to see Jeffrey, so Chris and a nurse wheeled me up to the NICU. When they finally put him in my arms I just couldn't believe it. He was such a handsome baby, with blond hair and blue eyes. We had done it! I had accomplished what I set out to do: My son was alive! The feeling that I had survived so that my son would live was incredible – something that's still difficult to describe. So many emotions ran through me. I felt gratitude to all the people who had prayed for both of us – especially my husband, my parents, and my siblings. I was grateful to Father Charbonneau. And above all, I was grateful to Grandma and God, who clearly worked together to make this miracle happen.

There were still a few issues to work out. For example, I couldn't breastfeed because of the radiation treatments. But I was thrilled to be holding my baby boy – and I didn't want to let go.

Jeff was small, of course, and a little jaundiced, but otherwise he was as healthy as a preemie could be. The first night he even managed to pull off his oxygen tubes; the nurses reassured Chris that this meant he was breathing well on his own. Despite his small size, he had long legs, which I teased Chris about. We joked that if I had gone full term, I would have delivered a giant.

I was in the hospital for two days, while Jeffrey stayed for a full week, until he started gaining weight. Leaving him was hard for Chris and me. We visited every day, staying with Jeffrey from the moment the NICU opened until the nurses kicked us out at night.

When Jeffrey reached five pounds, Dr. Mastrobattista said we could take him home. We had a special outfit picked out for Jeffrey for this wonderful day. It was a bit big on his tiny body, but I didn't care. I couldn't contain my excitement as we drove to the hospital to pick him up.

Chris and I had one minor issue before we could take Jeffrey home: We couldn't figure out how to put the car seat into the Suburban. We argued about it before securing the seat. In a way, we were acting like any other new parents. Everything felt almost normal again.

◊◊◊

I started chemotherapy in late June, a few weeks after Jeff was born. The treatment, popular at the time, involved a mixture of three drugs: Procarbazine, CCNU, and Vincristine. The so-called "PCV" or "trifecta" cocktail had proven effective in treating glioblastoma tumors, but Dr. Sawaya acknowledged that combining different drugs increases their potential toxicity, raising the risk of side effects like anemia or reduced platelet counts. I received the drugs in stages, in both pill form and intravenously. Each cycle lasted for three weeks, followed by a week off. Rest was key. I made it through five rounds. I was supposed to do six, but I just didn't have the energy to complete the final round.

After the chemo treatments ended, Dr. Groves put me on Accutane. I thought, *Acne medicine for cancer?* But oncologists doing research at MD Anderson had discovered that Accutane encourages immature cancer cells to die or stop dividing, minus the toxicity of traditional chemo drugs. So I took Accutane for a year after the initial chemotherapy ended. The side effect was that it severely dried out my skin. I had horrible problems with cracking on my lips and my nose.

Between the chemo and having a newborn, I needed a lot of help those first few months. It was a team effort. Mom stayed with me for a week, then went to Atlanta to help Heather, who had given birth to a second daughter, Jenelle, three weeks after Jeffrey was born. My cousin Kate, in college at the time, came down for the summer to help out. Chris called her "supernanny." Then my Aunt Moira (Mom's sister) visited from Maine for a week. After Aunt Moira left, we hired the wife of one of my associates at Beck Redden to be our in-home nanny for the rest of Jeff's first year.

Amid the chaos of those first few months, I became more appreciative of the little things. One of my favorite times of day was – and still is – the early morning, when I'm the first one awake, sipping a fresh cup of coffee and not yet thinking about the day ahead. Everything is so quiet, so peaceful. These are the times I reflect on my good fortune in having Grandma and God guide my son safely into this world.

Chapter 13

The New Normal

After Jeffrey was born, my focus was on getting back to "normal." Other than the fatigue that resulted from the chemo treatments, I felt fine physically. So in September 2003 I returned to work.

For a while, the routine worked. Chris and I were both busy, balancing our work schedules with Jeffrey's needs. Being a new lawyer, a new mom, a new wife, and a new cancer patient was overwhelming at times, and I probably overcommitted. But Chris and I started feeling normal again.

We traveled a lot. We took Jeff to New England in June 2004, where he saw his first Red Sox game (against the Yankees) in Fenway Park. Later that year, we visited Chicago and saw the Cubs play in Wrigley Field. Jeff's bedroom was full of both Red Sox and Cubs paraphernalia – a nod to the friendly rivalry between his mom's and dad's hometown teams!

During our trip to New England, we visited Maine, where Jeff saw the Atlantic Ocean for the first time and met his Great Grandma Winnie Hilton, who had lived in the same house in South Portland for a half century. Two years later, Winnie would be diagnosed with cancer. She and I would spend many hours on the phone, and in person during our vacation trips, talking about cancer and the right state of mind for fighting it – which she did, bravely, for five years. Winnie passed away on June 4, 2011, at the age of eighty-three.

In 2005 our next-door neighbors Stephanie and Tom Sikora invited Chris and I to Lake Tahoe, where the two of us skied together for the first time in eight years. (Our first time on the slopes didn't go so well. We were visiting Vermont for Thanksgiving and took a day to go skiing. Chris had frequently bragged about his ski trips as a kid in Wisconsin and in the Poconos. Those hills, however, did not prepare him for our trip to Sugarbush Resort in Vermont's Mad River Valley, where the trails were quite a bit steeper. Chris had to be assisted down the mountain on a sled by the Ski Patrol.) In Tahoe, the four of us skied for several days on the aptly named Heavenly Mountain. It was heavenly for sure, with amazing, sun-splashed views of the lake from the summit.

Back in Houston, other parts of our routine slowly fell into place. Chris and I golfed together – something we had done frequently from the first time we met. We watched movies with Jeffrey. We even watched the Red Sox win the World Series for the first time in eighty-six years! I was a long-suffering Red Sox fan like many others who grew up in New England. Most of us expected something bad to happen right up until that final Series-clinching game on October 27, 2004. I paced our living room, waiting for the last pitch that would end the dreaded Curse of the Bambino and bring us a world championship! I could not believe that the team actually won – and that I was able to see it happen. I proudly wore my Red Sox hat to work the next day.

As the months passed, Dr. Groves took me off more of my meds. I began feeling healthier and gradually began exercising again. Dr. Groves even gave me permission to pursue one of my bucket-list items: skydiving. Chris thought that jumping out of a plane would be too much for me. "You're acting like you're dying," he told me. I couldn't understand his frustration – I was fighting for everything I had, every day, and I simply wanted to accomplish the things I always dreamt of doing. In August 2004, Tim McGraw – my favorite country singer – released a song called "Live Like You Were Dying," which became my theme song. The song was about Tim's dad, former major league baseball pitcher Tug McGraw, who was diagnosed with brain cancer in 2003 and died nine months later. When I first heard the song, the lyrics – which spoke to all the things Tug did before he passed away – stopped me in my tracks.

To this day, the song reminds me how lucky I am to still be here. Sometimes when I hear it, I'll call Mom and ask her to visit, or text Chris to see how his day is going. Or I'll simply tell Jeff how much I love him. The song is a reminder that unexpected things sometimes happen, but no matter how tragic the situation, you have to keep going – and live like you were dying. And that's a good thing.

I haven't been skydiving yet – but it's still on my list.

◊◊◊

Cancer remained the one unfortunate part of our everyday lives. It affected my family in different ways on different days. I went through stretches where I was tired and still had headaches – normal for most people but always a cause for concern for me. There were a few other scares along the way. In mid-2004, an MRI showed a spot in my front left lobe, behind my left eye. The doctors were concerned because the growth was in front of the original tumor. The three physicians who reviewed the tests couldn't agree on whether the growth was a tumor or necrosis, which is dead tissue that can form following radiation treatments. It was difficult for them to distinguish between the two with an MRI because the area looked like a series of clouds.

Dr. Groves was frustrated. At one point, he was so mad he slammed the test results onto the floor of the examination room. He scheduled another MRI for a month later, and the follow-up indicated that the spot had become much smaller – though it looked like it was solidifying. Eventually, the doctors felt confident that the growth was necrosis. We all breathed a big sigh of relief.

A year later, I had a minor seizure at work. The EMTs came and took me to MD Anderson, where I went through another full battery of tests, which thankfully turned out negative. After the episode, I began taking anti-seizure medication.

Those events took their toll on the entire family. Chris was always on edge about my health. Any virus or odd reaction to a bug bite set off alarms. We made a lot of trips to the emergency room. He kept waiting for the bubble to pop.

Through it all, I remained focused on Jeff. Every time I watched him smile, learn something knew, show a new part of his personality, I would hate my cancer all over again. I struggled with the possibility that I wouldn't see him grow to be a toddler, a teen, a man.

◊◊◊

Jeffrey grew fast – lengthwise at least. By his first birthday he had reached the seventy-fifth percentile in height, although his weight was still in the fifteenth. He was tall and thin like his dad. At eighteen months he called me "Mommy" for the first time. Two months later he finally said his own name – which he pronounced "Yeffy."

We all survived Jeff's Terrible Twos, which lived up to their name. By his third birthday, Jeff had firmly established his independence. "No, Mommy, I'm gonna do it" became one of his favorite phrases. But he also enjoyed helping others. "I'll get that for you, Mommy!" he would say with enthusiasm. It was clear early on that Jeff was very smart. His intelligence was both a blessing and a curse. If he wasn't challenged he quickly became bored, which usually led to outbursts. But it was nothing that "normal" parents couldn't handle.

The list of "firsts" Jeffrey experienced grew: his baptism at St. Mary Magdalene Catholic Church in Humble; his first Houston Texans football game; playing in his first soccer game (he did great); swimming by himself in the pool; starting kindergarten.

Still focused on returning to normalcy, Chris and I talked about expanding our family. I was too high-risk to attempt another pregnancy, but both of us desperately wanted Jeff to have a brother or sister. We looked into surrogacy and met with several potential surrogates in 2005. My cousin Kate, bless her heart, offered to donate her eggs. We came close a few times to choosing a surrogate. In 2006 we had a verbal agreement with a woman to be a carrier, but we could never close the deal. A mix of contractual, insurance, and other issues created barriers that we ultimately couldn't overcome.

We turned our attention to adoption. Throughout 2007 we explored options in the U.S. and Russia. The timelines for the process were terrible – months of waiting and red tape. Chris grew increasingly frustrated and kept asking how much longer we wanted to keep at it.

I continued to hope that something would work out. I prayed every day and "talked" with Grandma frequently. She kept telling me that everything was going to be okay. At times it was hard for me to be sure if I was really talking to an angel or just hearing things that I wanted to hear.

◊◊◊

My responsibilities gradually increased at work, culminating in what I had desperately yearned for: hands-on trial experience. In February 2006 I spent five weeks in San Antonio as part of the defense team for ExxonMobil in a $100 million fraud case. It was incredible, but exhausting. A month later, I had my first opportunity to argue a motion on my own before a judge. Chris helped me prepare by having us watch a couple of episodes of *Boston Legal* – the drama in which William Shatner played a lawyer named Denny Crane. When I stood in front of the judge, I tried to channel my inner Shatner! I must have done all right, because the judge denied the opposing motion. Later that year, I worked a *pro bono* case for a family displaced by Hurricane Katrina.

I was really proud of what I accomplished in those cases and others that followed. But I was struggling, personally and professionally, to keep up the pace. My cognitive skills were not improving. I was having trouble finding the right words in my written and verbal communications. Good writing was one of my strengths when I was hired, but my skills were deteriorating. My colleagues were frustrated by my forgetfulness and my sometimes-sloppy work. One day, one of the firm's partners called me into his office to look over something I had written for him the day before. Re-reading it, I realized how terrible the report was. In one section I had started a sentence but never finished it. I started crying in his office.

Chris's frustrations increased even more. He told me to start carrying a small piece of paper and pen in my pocket or purse so I could write down the things I needed to do each day. My frustrations also grew. Those old childhood feelings that I wasn't living up to my potential returned. I needed help.

I began some brain therapy sessions at MD Anderson's Management and Interventions for Neurocognitive Dysfunction (MIND) Clinic, a neuropsychology center for cancer survivors.

The testing revealed that I had lost some short-term memory functions, which the therapists lovingly called "in one ear and out the other syndrome." I also had trouble translating thoughts to written words. Unfortunately, that skill was a critical part of my work as a lawyer when analyzing cases and preparing written arguments.

I was thankful for the testing, because it showed that I was not intentionally slacking off. But regardless of the cause, I didn't want to be a "C" player. I worked with the MIND Clinic therapists on ways to more or less retrain my brain to find another home for those cognitive functions. The sessions helped me to re-establish some of the reading and writing foundations I had before my surgery and the treatments that followed. I also made some adjustments at work, like dictating my reports instead of trying to write them on the computer.

Unfortunately, the brain exercises didn't get me all the way back to "A" player status.

I started emotional therapy along with the occupational therapy, because I needed to come to grips with leaving my "old" life behind and accepting the "new" me. I had to make some choices about the parts of my life that were most important. The ones I kept coming back to were being Jeffrey's mom and being Chris's wife, followed closely by beating cancer. Practicing law ended up a distant fourth.

I needed a better schedule, a better diet, a better lifestyle. Everything I was trying to balance – work, MIND Clinic, raising a child, being a wife – had become too much to handle. There were times when I felt like I was spinning around in a giant hamster ball that never slowed down. As soon as I felt like I had established a good balance, things would start spinning out of control again.

I had been determined to become a lawyer since I was a chubby little girl in Colchester, Vermont. I busted my ass to lay the groundwork for my dream job. And I had nailed it. I was making a salary higher than I ever could have imagined – a long way from when I had to ask Mom for help paying the bills as I pinched every penny through law school. I still believe I would have been an incredible lawyer, but getting there now was putting too much strain on the more important things in my life. In May 2007, I took a leave of absence from Beck Redden. It was a horrible day.

◊◊◊

Surprisingly, I didn't miss work. I let go of a lot of stress when I left the firm. But I still had plenty to keep me busy and happy, like picking up Jeff from school every day and spending more time reading to him and playing with him. I was also able to spend more time with the rest of my immediate and extended family. My priorities certainly changed – as they do for most first-time moms, and most cancer survivors, for that matter. It's cliché, but simple things became more meaningful – going to a movie with Chris, singing with Jeff in the car while driving him to school, making dinner for all of us.

My love for music grew. Music can brighten a bad day. It can relax you in times of stress. Music can get you through the tough times and let you enjoy the best times even more. I encouraged Jeffrey to listen to it, dance to it, and play it. I sang to him whenever I could. Chris and I traveled to Cincinnati to see James Taylor in concert. I visited Heather in Atlanta, and we went to a Madonna concert. Both shows were amazing.

I'd been eager to see Madonna ever since the seventh grade when I first fell in love with her music. Her live performance touched my heart. At the end of the concert, a message on the

Jumbotron in the arena proclaimed: "Re-invent yourself." The message was exactly what I needed to hear. I needed to reinvent myself – because I was no longer ready to die.

Chapter 14

Not Dead Yet

A funny thing happened to this terminal cancer patient: I didn't die. Three months became three years. My thirties somehow stretched into my forties. I realized you can never predict what will happen next in life. After all, no one expected me to survive. Even Dr. Sawaya admitted that he was surprised at my recovery. He says that considering the type of tumor I had, it "truly is remarkable" that I've made it this far with the capabilities I still have. Other people I've met along the way haven't been as fortunate. Michael Kemp, the man who Dr. Sawaya operated on just before me on New Year's Eve in 2002, died in 2004. Many other friends I met during my journey, who had the same or similar brain cancer as me, have also passed. I have attended many of their funerals, and it hurts deeply when I hear of the death of a fellow cancer patient. We all had a special bond. I often wonder, Why did they die when I told them all to keep fighting? I still haven't figured out why they've gone to heaven while I'm still here. I hope to see them all again when it is my time to go.

I did some interviews in the first couple of years following my surgery and Jeff's birth. The local Fox affiliate in Houston did a story about me and my "miracle baby," and I spoke on a few panels at MD Anderson. At the first panel, in early 2005, I was nervous, but I enjoyed telling my story. The doctors had arranged for Chris's mom, Margo, to bring Jeff into the room after I spoke. He was a good little salesman. As he walked in he smiled and waved. He was a wonderful inspiration to everyone.

I love sharing my story with other cancer patients and their families. My message to them is generally simple: Good and bad things happen in life; there's no way around it. But the open support of family can have a positive impact on a person's ability to deal with cancer and its many challenges.

Sometimes, based on my emotions at the time, I worry that I won't be positive enough to inspire others to fight the good fight. At times it was hard to explain to others what I was going through emotionally and physically. Friends and family would say that they "understood" – but there was no way anyone could understand what the cancer had done to me. I didn't want advice. I wanted encouragement and support. I didn't need someone to say, "Here's what you should do …" Instead, I needed someone to say, "You *will* get through this – I have complete faith in you, Tracey. You can do it. If you need me, I'll be there for you, no questions asked." I wondered at times who had faith in me, and who really thought I would survive.

I was frustrated trying to figure out why God decided he needed me here. What was it I was supposed to be doing? The best way I could answer that question was to remember my blessings and pass them along to others. One night, I shared my uncertainty with Chris. "Why am I still here?" I asked. He responded by simply pointing his finger – first at Jeff, then back at himself. He was right. I was there for them. At times I grew tired of dealing with cancer – all the tests, all the meds, the fatigue and the forgetfulness. Without my family, I probably would have given up.

◊◊◊

Chris and I continued to explore adoption. In mid-2007 we were at the top of the list for an adoption in Nevada, with a mother who was four months pregnant but didn't plan to keep her baby girl. Chris was concerned that the timing was off because I'd stopped working, but we moved ahead.

As with our surrogacy attempts, the adoption became a long, drawn-out, and ultimately devastating process. So many things we requested weren't completed, including an amniocentesis that we paid for in advance for the mother to ensure the baby's health. The adoption fell through in early July, when the birth mother had second thoughts. A few days later, the social worker called and said the mother had changed her mind *again*, and the adoption was back on. The baby was due on October 31, and as the date approached, I got more and more excited. Chris was nervous and a little doubtful; he was so scared that I was going to die and leave him with two small children to care for on his own.

In August we flew to Las Vegas to meet the birth mom in person. We brought a check as a deposit to secure the adoption. We met for coffee and accompanied her to an appointment with the obstetrician. Everything remained on track – until a few weeks before the due date, when we learned that the mother had tested positive for crystal meth. This made it likely that the baby would be born with a variety of physical and psychological ailments. Given my situation, there was no way I would be able to care properly for a baby who needed such long-term care. We walked away. I was heartbroken.

We finally decided that adding to our family was simply not meant to be.

◊◊◊

The failed adoption only increased Chris's fears and frustrations. Goodness knows I had my own. We often took our frustrations out on each other. There were times when I felt Chris didn't respect me as a woman, as a professional, as a mother, and as a wife. In his eyes, nothing I did was positive. In my mind, I was a complete failure. We would get upset with each other for little things, like me bouncing a check because I forgot to transfer money from one account to another, or him not picking up milk on the way home. Worst of all, we stopped offering the love and friendship we had when we first met. We each pushed the other further and further away.

Small problems often turned into bigger ones because we weren't communicating well. We began fighting regularly, over big things and little things, too often in front of Jeff. We were still together but we both felt alone. Cancer changed us both more than we were willing to admit. I prayed every day for us to figure out a better way to deal with our marriage.

I often wondered whether Chris wished that I hadn't survived so he could move on with his life. There were days when I was ready to wish him good luck on his journey (my way of saying "fuck you"!) and send him on his way. But I didn't, because I know that marriage is hard – in many ways, it proved harder than my fight with cancer. I still look at my parents and wonder how they did it. They survived their own cancer scares – Mom with breast cancer and Dad with prostate cancer – but they stayed strong, with and for each other. In 2004 our family traveled back to Vermont, where Mom and Dad renewed their vows to honor their thirty-five years of marriage. It was beautiful.

I married Chris because he was my best friend. I loved doing anything and everything with him. Traveling, boating, golfing, going to the movies, watching him play basketball with Jeff. He was always someone I could talk to about friends, family, or work. Chris gave me confidence and determination and made me feel like I was beautiful, treasured, smart, and someone he liked spending time with, all from the very first time we met on July 15, 1996. He is my true love, and I would do anything for him – and I always felt that he would do the same for me.

We had been through so many massive changes in our life together. But our marriage never became what either of us thought it would be – because of my cancer. We had trouble finding common ground. "You've become such a different person," he told me. He didn't know how or what to feel or expect from me or our marriage. In my mind, however, I was the same person. I just no longer had the same tools I had five years earlier. I tried so hard to find my way and still be the confident and independent lady I was so proud to be the day I married Chris.

My respect and love for Chris didn't change, but our friendship and care for one another did. We tried hard to fix it. I wanted to take his pain away and get back what we once had. But the void grew. We continued to criticize each other for not taking care of one another. Those old feelings that I wasn't good at anything kept creeping back into my mind.

My cancer changed what I was to Chris – still strong, but not the lady he married. Cancer takes an immeasurable toll on the caregivers. Death brings them indescribable pain – but if, by the grace of God, the patient lives, the caregivers face a new set of challenges. Friends and family always asked Chris how Jeff and I were doing, but rarely did they ask Chris how he was holding up. Caregivers often need just as much support as the patients themselves. They need time to decompress and share their feelings. Had I known that, perhaps things would have ended differently for Chris and me.

Ultimately, we cut holes in the fabric of our relationship that we were never able to mend. We divorced in December 2011.

Chapter 15

Truly Blessed

Families may be large or small, related by blood or formed by friendship and respect. Family members don't always get along, but the concept of family is an incredible blessing to protect and value. Time as a family has and always will be the most important part of my life. This is something my grandmother, Theresa Reid O'Regan, showed us all through her words, her actions, and her sacrifices.

I thank God every day for my gift, for the strength and determination that has led me to where I am today. To go out to dinner with Jeff, to watch him play with his friends, to hear him tell me about his day – I never take these moments for granted. They make me appreciate what Grandma did for me personally, but also for my family. I am truly blessed. I have plenty of bad days, but I know enough to take hold of every good day, store it, remember it, write about it, and share it with others.

Through the years Jeffrey has continued to amaze me, make me smile, and remind me every day of how lucky Chris and I were to have received this blessing from God. During a visit to Vermont a few years ago, Jeff and I were having breakfast at our hotel. An elderly woman came up to our table and said she'd been watching us. "I just wanted to let you know how impressed I am with the way your son is behaving," she said. "You're doing a wonderful job setting limits for him, but you're still smiling and having fun." It was one of my proudest moments as a mother.

Jeff has continued to flourish. He's a smart, good-looking, athletic, and truly loving young man with a constant desire to be at the top of everything he does. I see all of these traits in him every day – along with his stubbornness and desire to be in control of everything all the time! He can certainly be a handful, especially when he gets bored. But he is and always will be my true inspiration in this cancer fight. Without Jeffrey, I don't know where I would be today.

My MRIs have stayed clean since the necrosis scare in 2004. I'm only tested once a year now. I'm still considered "terminal," but when I turned forty I felt I'd reached a turning point. Instead of the end, I was beginning one of the most significant and brilliant times of my life.

Doctors and scientists continue to make progress in the fight against cancer. My spirits were lifted in early 2015 when I watched a report on *60 Minutes* about researchers at Duke University who had been experimenting with a new treatment for glioblastoma. The clinical trial involved injecting the brain tumors with polio – a seemingly crazy idea, but one that has proven effective in killing glioblastoma cells. Of the twenty-two patients in the trial, eleven have died, but the other half has shown improvement, with four patients in remission.

Watching the broadcast, I was stunned. I called my parents and then Chris to tell them the story. We shared some tears, and a sense of relief. Could doctors really find a cure for glioblastoma in my lifetime? I hope and pray that this treatment works.

I don't feel Grandma's presence as often these days. Maybe it's because I don't need her guidance as much anymore. But I know for certain that for the past thirteen years, "Toiréasa" – the harvester – has been watching over me. I often think back to Grandma's last days, how our family spent time gathered at her hospital bedside as she prepared herself for death. How she decided to trade places with me. In many ways, those final days captured Grandma's essence. As family and friends paid their respects and said their goodbyes, Grandma was alternately witty and reflective. "There's always someone watching you," she said at one point, "and they're a reflection of everything you do."

Given her love of language, it's not surprising that Grandma spent her final hours philosophizing about words. "There are boxes filled with words, and one box holds a universal word," she said. "And when you find that word, it will explain everything you need to know."

I don't have boxes filled with words, but I do have several journals. A year after Jeffrey was born, I began writing to him. I had no idea how long I would live, and I wanted him to know a little about who I was – just in case I wasn't around to raise him. In truth, the letters weren't just for Jeff. Putting my feelings down on paper was very important to me personally. Writing helped me through the changes in my life after the brain surgery. It helped me accept some changes, be more patient with family and friends, and settle into a life that I never would have wished for or imagined.

This book is an extension of those journals, and another way for me to share my experiences and give hope to others who are battling cancer. Faith is not a concept that I thought a lot about or really understood until I was diagnosed with brain cancer. But now I understand. Faith means believing that hard work and determination will pay off. Faith means knowing that people will care for you when you need it most. As a Catholic, faith means praying to God and to my grandmother. I encourage everyone – Catholic or not – to pray when you need a lift.

This book is another milestone in what has turned into my personal marathon. This final chapter is not an epilogue – I see it as more of a foreward. Because that's the way I'm looking at life. Always forward.

It's only fitting that since Jeffrey was the inspiration for my writing – for my life – my closing words should be to him.

Jeffrey

I love you "to the moon and back."
Thank you for your smile,
It is magical.
Your independence
It is important.
Your love
Helps me every day.
Thank you for keeping me strong,

You are my shining star
A strong and caring Young Man.
I am so proud of you
Like most mothers are of their sons.

Faith in yourself
Will always send you to the right place.

Your star is always rising –
Don't forget to keep looking up.
You will end up exactly where you are meant to be.

Always, your Mom